I0761515

# EL MUNDO ZURDO 6

## SELECTED WORKS FROM THE 2016 MEETING OF THE SOCIETY FOR THE STUDY OF GLORIA ANZALDÚA

EDITED BY
SARA A. RAMÍREZ,
LARISSA M. MERCADO-LÓPEZ,
AND SONIA SALDÍVAR-HULL

*aunt lute books*

*San Francisco*

Copyright ©2018 by the Society for the Study of Gloria Anzaldúa

All rights reserved. This book, or parts thereof, must not be reproduced in any form or by any means, electronic or mechanical, including photocopying and recording, or by an information storage and retrieval system, without written permission from the publisher.

Archival material on pages 32 and 33 reprinted by permission of the Gloria E. Anzaldúa Literary Trust.

Aunt Lute Books
P.O. Box 410687
San Francisco, CA 94141
www.auntlute.com

Cover design: Amy Woloszyn, Amymade Graphic Design
Cover art: "New Moon: (Re)learning the Way Back Home," Ramona Garcia ©2016
Text design: Amy Woloszyn, Amymade Graphic Design
Senior Editor: Joan Pinkvoss
Managing Editor: Shay Brawn
Production: Andrea Ikeda, Maya Sisneros, Kari Simonsen, Katie O'Brien, and Samantha Marley Barnett

Library of Congress Cataloging-in-Publication Data

Names: Mundo Zurdo (Conference) (6th : 2016 : University of Texas at San Antonio) | Ramírez, Sara A., editor. | Mercado-López, Larissa M., editor. | Saldívar-Hull, Sonia, 1951- editor.
Title: El Mundo Zurdo 6 : selected works from the 2016 Meeting of the Society for the Study of Gloria Anzaldúa / edited by Sara A. Ramírez, Larissa M. Mercado-López, and Sonia Saldívar-Hull.
Description: San Francisco : Aunt Lute Books, [2018] | Includes bibliographical references.
Identifiers: LCCN 2018015954 | ISBN 9781879960978 (alk. paper)
Subjects: LCSH: Anzaldúa, Gloria--Philosophy--Congresses. | Anzaldúa, Gloria--Influence--Congresses. | Anzaldúa, Gloria--Study and teaching--Congresses. | Women's studies--Congresses. | Identity (Psychology)--Congresses. | Creation (Literary, artistic, etc.)--Congresses. | Minorities--Education--Congresses. | Hispanic Americans--Education--Congresses. | Borderlands--Social aspects--Congresses. | Mexican-American Border Region--Social conditions--Congresses.
Classification: LCC PS3551.N95 Z78 2016 | DDC 818/.5409--dc23
LC record available at https://lccn.loc.gov/2018015954

Printed in the U.S.A. on acid-free paper
10 9 8 7 6 5 4 3 2 1

# CONTENTS

# EL MUNDO ZURDO 6

## SELECTED WORKS FROM THE 2016 MEETING OF THE SOCIETY FOR THE STUDY OF GLORIA ANZALDÚA

# LA BUTCHA BARBER

ANEL I. FLORES

she sees herself
in the mirror
sucks in a deep breath
absorbs the majesty

her brown bulging nipples
her pendulous breasts

steps back
grips fingers around the bulge of soft fat
pulls the boob up towards her chin
opens up her other hand
dropping a brown athletic band
rolling out onto the floor
past her feet
limp as a noodle
and presses the end of the fabric
where her triceps meets her pec
beneath the boob
still suspended

begins to feel her lungs fill with air
drops her arm
clipping the noodle between the pinch of her armpit
releases the droplet of skin

with the now-free hand,
she stretches the wrap over
both of her breasts
taut
under her opposite armpit
behind her back
compressing her breasts
as close to her ribcage as achievable

draws the athletic wrap
behind her back
tugging on it
until it snaps
the band emerges again from behind her armpit

she takes the leftover
repeats the wrapping
watches the hanging fabric
get shorter and shorter for each bind
through the reflection in the mirror

her posture uncurls
from its slouch
she stands up straight
the skin stings like a knee burn on caliche
her chichis are numb
obscure
hollow

she fills with air
steps forward
sure

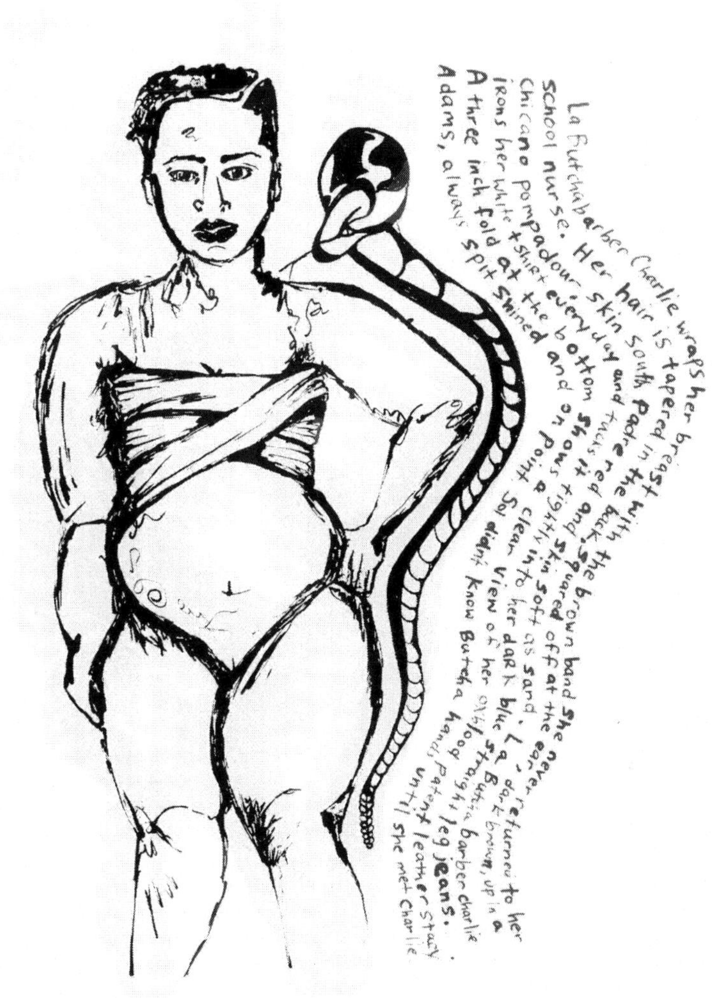

**LA BUTCHA BARBER**

Medium: Original Two-Color Serigraph
*Limited Edition of 25*
*Hand-Signed & Numbered*
*100% cotton archival paper*
*Printed by Malaquias Montoya at Taller Arte del Nuevo Amanecer*

# *ATRAVESANDO MUNDOS; ACORRALANDO TIEMPOS*

## *SOÑANDO CON SERPIENTES*

ALEJANDRA I. RAMÍREZ

> To awake, then, is to change how and what we remember.
>
> –Patrisia Gonzales, *Red Medicine* (2012)

> *Inconscientemente te he buscado*
> *Sombra*
> *En lo obscuro de mi soledad*
> *De noche*
> *Y de día*
> *Eres ánima fugaz.*
>
> –A.I.R.

This dream narrative begins, like many stories do, with unexplained phenomena, and so it is also a project that perhaps cannot be fully understood or should have remained untold. It weaves itself in and out of the shadows below or awake states. The unknowable and ineffable. Stories that precede but are beyond the scope of Western "logical" thinking. The home of dreams and imagination, and their transformational powers. The traces of memories, consciousness, and hopes.

Where infinite connections are interwoven. Where the language of symbols and visions come alive and move like a snake.

My work here is a practice in *dream autohistoria-teoría,* a theory in the flesh and in the psyche, a practice inspired by Gloria Anzaldúa and Cherríe Moraga's framework conceptualized in *This Bridge Called My Back* that helps to articulate everyday experiences as theory and legitimate epistemologies (19). In an act of expanding on this dreamwork as a theory in the flesh, I delve into the recesses of my wild psyche, my dreams and dreamscapes—the places we go to when our bodies go to sleep. I explain how dreams are also a legitimate place of knowing and can inform our scholarship and daily lives. That is to say, our dreams hold knowledge and information about the past, present, and future that can expand our understanding of what it means to *be*, ontologically speaking, even if that be-ing-ness is always already split into multiple ways of existing and knowing. Furthermore, the knowledge and experiences within those dreams have the potential to seep into other areas of one's life. In my case, a series of snake dreams have influenced my artwork and my research methods and methodologies as well as locations of inquiry.

In an effort to articulate my thinking about *epistemic decolonization through dream teoría,* I retell my experiences within a dream narrative, or a dreamer autohistoria, a theory that emerged from Patrisia Gonzales's course on traditional medicine at the University of Arizona. I make the connection with the particular dream and my process of developing dream teoría/autoteoría/autohistoria from the experience and the images of the serpent in my dream. Later, by linking theorists to the description of my dream experiences, I explain how applying decolonizing theories to concepts and interpretations of "vision" disrupt Western empiricist logics of what I/we can know (epistemology[1]) and who I am/we are (ontology). Nepantla and nagualismo, Anzaldúa explains, are the result of living within double vision or double consciousness, and result in the need to shapeshift depending on where we are and what we need to be. In *Light in the Dark/Luz en lo Oscuro*, Anzaldúa defines nepantla as "the place where my cultural and personal codes clash…the point of contact y el lugar between worlds—between imagination and physical existence, between ordinary and nonordinary (spirit) realities" (2).

I will begin by explaining serpentine/serpent methodology to describe my wayward thinking and writing. In so doing, I theorize the role that the serpent plays in spiritual and embodied knowing and being, a *mindbodyspirit* knowledge. I argue that these dreams and theories are aspects of an intuitive knowing, serpent and serpentine conocimientos that are also an aspect of my psyche and everyday physical world. In this essay, I also work with the term *traviesa* as a method to help make these links. After establishing this methodology, I will describe an account of a dream I had as well as recount a few others in order to think more deeply about what role these dreams play in my life and in my intellectual projects like my research, art, and poetry. I will build my argument that dreams are a location of legitimate knowledge, in essence an *episteme*, a theory or system of knowing. I finish by situating this dream autohistoria-teoría as a project in the process of decolonization because I believe spiritual and healing work is an act of resistance within academic conversations and spaces, what in "Now Let Us Shift" Anzaldúa calls "spiritual activism" (545).

## *VISIONES SERPENTINAS Y TRAVESURAS ARTÍSTICAS:* A SERPENTINE METHODOLOGY

> ...my vigilance, my thousand sleepless serpent eyes blinking in the night, forever open. And I am not afraid.
>
> –Gloria E. Anzaldúa (*Borderlands/La Frontera* 73)

First, let me begin my artist and dream critique by stating that I am a traviesa! Typically, traviesa or travieso is a term imposed on willful young children while they are in the beginning stages of their curiosity about the world. It is used as disciplining discourse through shaming children who are wayward, queer, or who have a variety of interests and attentions. As a child growing up on the extremities of Piedras Negras, Coahuila, Mexico, I chased chickens and would get lost in the woods. I wouldn't brush my hair and I would even cut it off, because to me it was (and continues to be) burdensome and unnecessary. I would talk to the wind and rest in small arroyos, letting the water run over me. It is in this childlike spirit that I approach my transdisciplinary academic work and abstract art forms. I play with multiple disciplines, genres, and theories that inform my experiences, curiosity, and thinking. I choose what feels right and if something isn't working out, I let it go. I see the snake, the serpent, as a traviesa as well. Both the serpent and I are traversing times and spaces in order to gain an understanding of the world in order to survive within it.

### *TRAVIESA: UNA FENOMENOLOGÍA*

Ser una traviesa significa estar consciente de las barreras y jaulas físicas y metafísicas que nos imponen los gobiernos y las culturas; esa consciencia critica de una traviesa que resulta en manifestaciones de rebeldía. The traviesa suffers as her spirit yearns to be unleashed and liberated of the boundaries that have cut her into pieces. Like Coatlicue and Coyolxauhqui, dismembered spiritually, historically, and physically.

A traviesa thoughtfully traverses: se atraviesa sobre fronteras, lenguas, y tradiciones. Una atravesada crosses even when she is afraid, and in that act of crossing (a travesura) exposes the limits and weaknesses of binaries, boundaries, and compartmentalization. In the *Borderlands/La Frontera* chapter "Movimientos de rebeldía y las culturas que traicionan," Anzaldúa articulates the responses from her family as she traversed boundaries of tradition, comportment, gender, sexuality, language, and movement (by leaving home) (38). *Terca*, stubborn, disobedient, they would call her. For Anzaldúa, her rebellion was her "Shadow-Beast." She writes:

> There is a rebel in me—the Shadow-Beast. It is a part of me that refuses to take orders from outside authorities. It refuses to take orders from my conscious will, it threatens the sovereignty of my rulership. It is that part of me that hates constraints of any kind, even those self-imposed. At the least hint of limitations on my time or space by others, it kicks out with both feet. Bolts. (38)

Traviesas are cunning and aware; they are skillful and know how to improvise. They are willful, and that strength in will is not often cherished in traditionalist families where women are raised to be docile and quiet. A traviesa understands this, and refuses silence.

The serpent is a traviesa, and it is from the emergence of travesuras in childhood that the playful connections between scholarship, dreams, and art can be permitted to coalesce in all their liveliness. My art and writing is like a travesura; a serpentine, wayward, often fractured, curious cartography of dreamscapes. A knowledge that precedes and transcends language. I've had many dreams of serpents since I was very young. Recently though, I've started to paint them and write about them more and more. Sometimes, I'll wake up at three in the morning or in the middle of the night, my body provoked to create. I have been painting my dreams for about a year now. I would like to talk a bit about the painting of a serpent, which emerged from the dream event. I've titled the painting *El Abrazo Infinito*, or the Infinite Embrace. The process of creating art, in direct relation to and provoked by the dreams, is also a spiritual process of awakening and understanding. This essay too is a project that emerged from these dreams.

*El Abrazo Infinito* depicts a diagonal/transverse, giant, dual-bodied serpent. It is made up of three large canvases stacked diagonally. At the center of the work is what we have come to know as Las Siete Cuevas, or Chicomóztoc. It is known as the origin of matter, the womb of the earth. In my painting, two snake heads touch and form Chicomóztoc and spiral outward onto the three panels. The green spiral/coiled serpent goes off the canvas and gives the appearance of going on infinitely. In the lower panel, the womb of Chicomóztoc bleeds into the underworld—underneath, under the waters, beneath the land. Birth has occurred already in this scene. In the top panel, there are clouds and lightning strikes connected to the clouds and to the ground. You see that one of the lightning strikes has shocked Chicomóztoc where the two serpent heads meet. The lightning bolt illuminates the two serpents and zigzags along the entirety of their bodies as they coil infinitely off the painting.

There is no beginning because there is no end. It is an instant, as quick as a lightning strike, that seems to animate the painting and the experiences in my dream that I cannot articulate in words or alphabetic language. This lightning represents the seizures my son had in the dream I will retell for you and the possible electric experience in my bed the night of the dream. I will explain the dream and the electricity in my experience and in my mindbodyspirit more in detail in a moment.

In one experience with serpentine or serpent dreams, I fell asleep and prayed for clarity as I worked through my understanding of why the snake kept appearing in my world (both dream world and "real" world). In this dream I was floating above a nest of snakes, and as I looked down I saw them moving as if they were a woven blanket in motion. When I woke up, I knew almost instantly that the theory of the serpent that I had been working on was not just about one snake, but rather many snakes. Everything that moves like a snake. The multiverse moves like a snake. Sound moves like a snake. Light waves move like snakes. Mountains, oceans, hills, rivers, echoes—all move like snakes. They're everywhere. The Milky Way looks like a giant snake. It became clear to me then why snakes are so prolific in ancient cultures from all over the world. I painted what I call "un lecho de serpientes," or "a nest of snakes." It is a series of brush-strokes that imitate serpentine movements. The painting includes one large and one small serpent, a heartbeat or heart rhythm, an octopus, and an umbilical cord. This painting, a theory of knowledge, represents the movements I kept seeing in my dreams and in the world around me—the many ways in which I received knowledge through all of my senses, including my dreams (as a place of sensorial possibilities).

The visual language of art and symbols are twins of dreamscapes. Irene Lara's "serpentine conocimiento" helps me articulate further my approaches to thinking and writing, in that serpentine conocimiento is "knowledge learned through *movimiento*, by moving back and forth, swishing side to side, moving through multidimensional space, spiraling" ("Sensing the Serpent" 116). It is a knowelge that has been passed on from our ancestors through stories, our dreams, and through sensing *through* the serpent—seeing, sensing, and knowing through the serpent spirit. Ancient cultures and ancestors from around the world have held an intimate relationship with snakes. Stories of serpent women and dieties are prolific, such as Medusa and Mami Wata, or in traditional healing practices such as placing a snake over the body to cure illness. Furthermore, Lara defines "serpentine conocimiento" as a consciousness that "centers knowledge and wisdom about and from the earthly and human-animal body—including conocimientos related to sex, sexuality, and the erotic" (116). Lara's theorizing and snake mythologies demonstrate innate knowledge as they are remembered with the entirety of one's being. In Greek philosophy, *anamnesis* refers to a knowldge system based on a belief that we are born possessing an innate understanding. Therefore, according to this Greek thought, we do not "discover" knowledge, but rather rediscover it.

While I understand the implications of including a Greek theory, specifically because of the imperialism of Western civilization, I believe there are possibilities for bridging multiple knowledge systems that can inform our understanding. In this case, the theory of anamnesis is helpful to understand the role of the serpent and other imagery in dreams and memory as innate knowledge. A shared consciousness of the power of dreams. Dreams inform us of a time and place before we were born—ancient knowledge communicated to us by the ancestors and the spirit world of the multiverse.

For this reason I argue that an ancient knowledge bursts onto canvases and keyboards, emerging from dreams, and made vivid by typed letters or strokes of a paintbrush.

Now, I'd like to tell you about my dream.

### *SUEÑOS SERPENTINOS*

This night was a full moon. Dreams shift shapes as the moon does, as our energies do.

It was mid–spring semester during a course with Dr. Patrisia Gonzales at the University of Arizona and I had been journaling my dreams for several nights. This evening, as my mother and I talked, her health came up, as it does in most of our conversations. We talked about manzanilla for her stomach and arnica for her swelling, and gordo lobo for her chest congestion. She was getting over a cold from another cold spring in Minnesota, and she has had problems with digestion for a while. I hung up the phone wanting to be closer to her; between me and her, though, time and geographical distance were the least of our problems.

I lay down on my stomach reading Cheryl Strayed's book *Wild: From Lost to Found on the Pacific Crest Trail*, a story of a young woman who loses her mother to cancer and embarks on an emotional and physical recovery on the long hike from the south US/Mexico border to the northern US/Canada border. Reading the story of the loss of Strayed's mother and after the conversation with my mother, I descended to the place in between where memories, wishes, and other impossibilities rest.

I looked out my bedroom window and saw the full moon. Something inside of me compelled me to speak words that still bring me to tears today. I asked my spirit to return to me; I called back my spirit. My words were intertwined with images of myself as a little girl, smiling, without a trouble in my heart—an innocent smile before the world made its mark on me. I asked that little spirit to come back, that I was ready for her to return.

I didn't know what I was saying or doing at the time, but I think that doing healing work is a science. Undoing years of trauma takes time, years even, to learn and to begin to heal. You try something to see if it will work, to see if it can work, or you try something different or repeat. One takes a chance, risks everything, for pure possibility. I've wanted so badly to feel the childhood joy that was taken from me so many years ago. I cried a little that night, put my book away, and said another prayer: I prayed that my dream tonight could guide me back to my spirit. I entered into my dreamworld and had two dreams this night. In the first, I saw and held my eldest son as he had two consecutive seizures. This was so frightening in my dream that I prayed to wake up, and I think I did but I cannot be sure.

At this point, I cannot tell you what is real or true in my account of what happened: neither my son nor I have ever experienced a seizure or anything of the sort before this, but in between being asleep and awake, I felt my entire body tighten and my muscles cramp up, and my torso rose off the bed and I felt myself trying to make a noise, like a groan. It was dark in my room, except for the moonlight—exactly what my room looked like before I went to sleep. Still, I found myself in my dreamscape, somewhere that I cannot explain.

In this dream, immediately after the seizure-like event in my bed, or perhaps during it, the snake appeared again for the second time in two weeks, and this time it was as if it was searching for me. It was a giant. It moved around skyscrapers, almost methodically or mechanistically. I was afraid. I have dreamed of snakes since I was young, either that a snake strikes at me, bites me, or crawls up my body, and I have always woken up at the point of contact. This time however, a child appears, non-gender-specific, with short hair, and they looked like my younger son. The non-gendered child had also been in my dreams before.

As I panic, the child touches me and points with their finger in the direction of a window far away. In the room with the window, on a table, sits a small clock.

I ask the child: "Will this stop time?" I wondered if it would stop the snake that was still looking for me. "No." The child responds, "It will only slow it down for short periods."

Then I woke up.

I opened my eyes to the bright Tucson morning sun, in a heavy sweat, my body aching and exhausted. I fell back asleep. In need of rest. The third time I fell asleep I did not dream. I rested. It was dark again.

## DECOLONIZING THEORIES/*TEORÍAS DESCOLONIZANTES*

While dreaming, theorizing, or writing alone will not undo or erase the trauma of capitalist patriarchy and racism, I offer my dream autohistoria and visions as a political act of resistance and refusal against traditional, Eurocentric academic expectations of assimilation that further seek to erase traditional knowledge and traditional medicine. I share my art and dream with you, as a dream/dreamer conveying my autohistoria-teoría, a la Anzaldúa, in order to better understand the role of dreams in our experience, consciousness, and healing. I gaze inward as an ethic of scholarly inquiry, which I believe has helped me to see and understand the world more broadly and intricately. In *Light in the Dark/Luz en lo Oscuro*, Anzaldúa describes autohistoria-teoría as "conectando experencias personales con realidades sociales…and theorizing about this activity" (6). Also, it is an attempt to understand the presence of the serpent or snake as an animal that has been appearing in my dreams since my early childhood.

In "Dreaming Ceremony: Medicine Dreams," Patrisia Gonzales explains that dreams are a form of "sacred sight," which comprise "original knowledge" (177). She writes that "dreams are both the site of knowledge and a way of knowing, as well as a method for organizing experience, interpreting data, and diagnosing illness and imbalance" (177). Furthermore, "dreaming is a simultaneous cocreative process that involves the bodyspiritland and life-moving powers in which there may or may not be borders between flesh, mind, spirit, cosmos, or place" (172).

Anzaldúa also dreamt of serpents. In "Entering into the Serpent," in *Borderlands/La Frontera*, she writes extensively about the distorted mythologies of serpents and their relationship to the feminine. She writes that the snake is "the symbol of the dark sexual drive, the chthonic (underworld), the feminine, the serpentine movement of sexuality, of creativity, the basis of all energy and life" (57). To Anzaldúa, la serpiente es su tono, her animal counterpart. For both Anzaldúa and Gonzales, dreams and serpents represent original knowledges, and ways of being and knowing in the world. Dreams are epistemologies and ontologies of healing and balance. For both, art is medicine and medicine is art.

As a curious person and graduate student, many questions arose for me because of this process. Most importantly: what is the potential of embracing the serpent and embracing dreams, both as a source of knowledge but also a tool of transformation and decolonization? How can this act of journaling our dreams and thinking/theorizing them heal ruptures and the deep soul wounds caused by violences and intergenerational trauma, pain that runs so deep that it's imbedded in our DNA and passed on to our children? I would like to consider what is possible when we open ourselves up, resist colonial violences against the imaginary and dream states, and delve deeply into the symbolism of our dreams and imagination, the place of darkness, the unknown, the intuitively sensed, collective unconscious of everything that is, was, and can be.

Dream places are also a nepantla stage. In "Now Let Us Shift," Anzaldúa reminds us that nepantla is "the overlapping space between different perceptions and belief systems" (541) and describes the "reptilian eye" in the middle of the forehead as the organ that allows one to see or sense within the nepantla space. She evokes the shapeshifting naguala: *the perceiver of shifts*, the one capable of sensing inward and outward transmogrifications simultaneously, the animus that will help us during the stages of conocimiento. In "Now Let Us Shift," Anzaldúa describes "la naguala" as "the function that arouses the awareness that beneath individual separateness lies a deeper interrelatedness" (569). Crisis ensues when we cling too dearly to an all-too-human ego that has been indoctrinated to rely on empirical evidence to determine truth and validity of knowledge and experience.

Also in "Now Let Us Shift," Anzaldúa continues to work with the definition of nepantla as the places where one struggles "to find equilibrium between the outer expression of change and your inner relationship to it" (549). This project tries to answer how dreams are also a place of nepantla, where invisible forces teach one to communicate with the spiritual world and our own inner worlds. The dream landscape may be a location of innate knowledge, the recess, perhaps, where "primal collective memory" dwells (Castillo 17). Throughout the ancient cultures of the world, the relationship between dreams and animal spirits has been a source of foresight and information. For me, serpents (and owls) have guided me in and outside of my dreams. I imagine the serpents moving around my world and try to see through their eyes, sense through their skin, enter their mouths, be bitten by them, talk to them through the only language we can agree on, which is the visual and instinctual, the language of dreams.

I have become obsessed with the serpent, and often wake in my dreams needing to draw, write or paint a serpent image or poem. I am compelled to create from an instinctual impulse I feel throughout my entire body. A restlessness. I often manifest the movement of the serpent on the canvas. My arms move in cyclical motions and I have also felt as though I am going into a trance state where my mind is completely empty but my body continues to create. This connection to art is an area I would like to think through as a projection and provocation of this process of understanding and healing. Traditional medicine teaches us that everything is medicine. I have come to understand that also the difficulties of birthing children, of parenting, of being a graduate student, as well as the difficulties of family relationships are medicine too, just as much as creosote, yerba buena, sage, and lemongrass are. Art and dreams have been the most important medicine for me thus far. My dreams have guided me and continue to guide my vision of the world.

According to Gonzales, among the Quiche, dreams can be understood through a lightning energy that is contained in a person's blood and muscles and announced as a bolt of energy that travels in the body. Furthermore, she explains:

> The spirit world, including dream knowledge systems, is considered to be imparted through the human anatomy as not only the soul of the mind but part of the vital energy of the blood (or the breath in other Nahua healing cosmologies). (179)

Seizures are described as a surge of electrical activity in the brain. I would encourage us to allow that collective lightning to speak through us day after day.

I do not claim tribal affiliation, nor do I have extensive knowledge of traditional medicine, nor can I know the degree to which Indigenous and First Nation people struggle for land, recognition, and dignity. I can only tell my stories, my family history of dispossession, forced migration, sexual and physical abuse, and abandonment. I vividly remember my grandmother's limpias and barridas over my young body with yerbas that scratched my skin and cold eggs she would crack open into a glass of water, para curar el "ojo" (asi le decían a alguien que se enfermó porque le "hicieron ojo," algo que también le dicen "el mal de ojo"), described as negative energy that sticks to someone through a jealous or evil gaze, "an evil eye." My grandmother, who is very old now, has lost much of her physiological eyesight.

Colonization has many faces and many tongues, and one of them is used to distort our senses and our sense of belonging. My grandmother tells me she is the daughter of Kickapoo parents. She worked primarily with plants and held winter/Christmas ceremonias. I remember her neighbors and family would come to our house for help and healing. She also taught my mother, who through her and my father's practices, taught my siblings and me the limited knowledge they knew. Through the process of connecting with my family and elders to learn about our family knowledgeways, I have also learned that my great grandfather communicated with the owls. Gonzales's "Mexican Traditional Medicine" class helped me to make these reconnections and visions more tangible. I was deeply moved by the course and her presence. I cannot grasp my entire history because we have been cut at an artery of our truths, but I have no doubt about what I have sensed on my flesh and my psyche and what has been passed on to me through my family members.

The treachery of colonization and its logics of disciplinarity, along with its partnering enforcer, heteropatriarchy, have *feminized* and attempted to render invisible the traditional ways of knowing—epistemologies that are inextricably tied with the land and natural phenomena, such as the movement of the stars, tides, sensuality, and dreams. Inquiring about the depths to which these colonizing logics impact our psyches, dreams, and imaginations moves women of color theorists and educators to unpack these locations of knowledge. My guiding curiosity and resulting queries about this ongoing project are centered around the broad concept of "vision," not only as a sensorial and physiological experience. My ongoing questions are concerned with the relationship between imagination, consciousness or cognition (*conocimiento*), and the way we understand the world that we *see*, both through direct physiological oculi as well as through the lenses of ideology. Furthermore, how both physiological and ideological *vision/s* have been impacted by colonization. Again, just some of the methods I engage with are through art, symbol, and dream analysis. The purpose of this (ongoing) project is to further fulfill my obsession with snakes as well as to understand the connection we have with our vision/s.

I play with serpent consciousness and transgressive methodologies because what has traditionally been deemed scholarly is too disciplining for me. As a firm believer in the possibilities of an oppositional, anti-colonial consciousness, I would like you to consider dream landscapes and trancing experiences as the fertile soil of epistemological ruptures in colonial, institutional spaces. I *play* here with theories lived through art, music, and symbols or words, not in the academic tradition, but rather with untraditional, untamed curiosity and intellectual liberty. I ask that you imagine that anything is possible, and that everything is medicine.

I return to Anzaldúa's nepantla consciousness and nagualismo often. I think about the ways our dreamscapes are a nepantla state-of-being and a place/location of being, a dynamic and real place between the spiritual and the embodied world. Anzaldúa's descriptions of nepantla as "the overlapping space between different perceptions and belief systems" (541), a site "where the outer boundaries of the mind's inner life meet the outer world of reality" (544), and as "the site of transformation, the place where different perspectives come into conflict" (548) speak to the inbetweenness of dreamscapes. Furthermore, nagualismo in dream autohistoria teoría suggests that one has the ability to perceive "something from two different angles" which "creates a split in awareness" (549). The naguala, is, after all, a shapeshifter and "perceiver of shifts" (542). This dreamscape and place of knowing is also a place of transformation if one is open to receiving the visions and images with serious attention. There are those who do not remember their dreams, or do not dream.

As Anzaldúa argues, those who have sought dreams as dimensions of knowledge, such as dream readers or card readers, have been *feminized* and demonized, processes that discredit and delegitimize these knowledgeways that relate to dreams and our relationships with the animal and natural worlds (543). Gonzales writes that "knowledge is experienced with the whole of our being" (xvii); one learns pain like one learns an alphabet or symbol system. It is stamped into our mindbodyspirit. I am curious to understand what a people learn through colonization, and how that impacts their physiological eyes as well as their spiritual sight, but more urgently, how to decolonize on that mind-bodyspirit level. Continents and people around the world have been subject to the violent Catholic and Christian religions partnered with patriarchy, tyranny, and imperialism, which have attempted to violently eradicate traditional Indigenous knowledgeways. It is for this reason that I argue that this project is an act of spiritual resistance, decolonization, and possibly reclaiming knowledge (in an intellectual or academic sense, at least).

I consider spiritual, dream, and animal visions (among many other ways of knowing/knowledgeways) as normative sources of information about ourselves and the multiverse, and as an epistemological imperative within decolonial thinking. In order to decolonize, we must do so on the level of our unconscious. Our dreams have much to teach us, warn us, and remind us about who we are, were, and can be. Informed also by Gonzales's *Red Medicine* and traditional dream knowledge and ceremonies, I answer the urgent incitement to decolonize what Western education teaches us about vision and dreams on an epistemic level, through artistic and methodological disruptions.

This process of thinking about dreams and writing about my own dream narratives and dream teoría has helped me articulate questions about what possibilities emerge about ourselves and our place in the multiverse. Putting into words what happens in my dreams has taught me about theory and methodology in ways that no other book on those terms has. Theorizing about serpents has led me to creative and complex methodologies. I continue to ask questions about the practice of *listening* to our dreams and *trusting* them. How can a dream autohistoria teoría challenge but expand on predominantly Western bodies of knowledge primarily concerned with "objectivity" and empiricism? What can we learn by thinking through dreams as a *situated knowledge*, an understanding that our collective minds, bodies, spirits, and visions are not distanced from one another but are responsive to and responsible for one another, what

Donna Haraway describes as "feminist objectivity"? (581) What is the potential of inquiring about our dreams as we would a poem, a painting, or a book as epistemological and ontological locations of memory, self- or collective understanding, and perhaps future knowings? How does thinking about our dreams as visions of a future tense help expand our current descriptions of vision and visionary work, about futurity and cultural memory, as we expand our understanding of how we "see"?

Nepantla, nagualismo, and dream ceremony are connected networks of understanding. I see these ways of thinking/theories as helpful not only because they explain double or split consciousness (*conocimiento*) but because they are theories that infinitely reveal the ever-shifting cosmic and ecological geographies of time and space. In other words, theories que *atraviesan mundos y tiempos*. For Anzaldúa and others, this awareness is represented in our dreams and may materialize as an animal counterpart, perhaps a *serpent*, an archetypal symbol of the natural and cosmic phenomenon of interdependence. Through a recent dreaming ceremony in which I experienced the serpent and symbols of time and the universe, as well as my creation of art as ceremony, I have called on the relationship with dreams of the serpent I've had since my childhood to explain how my consciousness is not only split in two but is, in fact, actively multiplying and regenerating every time I, a queer mujer and mother of color, encounter different temporalities and locations of knowing—whether that be my dreams, "reality," other countries, memories of childhood traumas, or any present moment in which it is necessary for me to be aware of and learn from my surroundings. These dream ceremonies and thinking iluminan mi camino. My hope is that this project encourages us all to dream. Write down our dreams. Listen to the images and visions of our (collective) imaginings.

## NOTES

1. The uses and definition of epistemology in this essay are informed by the work of Patrisia Gonzales in her book *Red Medicine* (2012) as she describes traditional Indigenous knowledge as dynamic, pluralistic, and embodied as knowledge is "experienced with the whole of our being" (xvii). She describes the "multiple dimensions of knowledge" to include place, correspondence, orientations, sacred formulas, ceremony as medicine, unity, explanation, embodiment, and memory (xx–xxiv).

## WORKS CITED

Anzaldúa, Gloria. *Borderlands/La Frontera: The New Mestiza.* 4th ed., Aunt Lute Books, 2012.

---. *Light in the Dark/Luz en lo Oscuro: Rewriting Identity, Spirituality, and Reality*, edited by Analouise Keating, Duke UP, 2015.

---. "now let us shift…the path of conocimiento…inner work, public acts." *this bridge we call home: radical visions for transformation*, edited by Gloria E. Anzaldúa and Analouise Keating, Routledge, 2002, pp. 540–78.

Castillo, Ana. *Massacre of the Dreamers: Essays on Xicanisma*, Plume, 1994.

Gonzales, Patrisia. *Red Medicine: Traditional Indigenous Rites of Birthing and Healing*, U of Arizona P, 2012.

Haraway, Donna. "Situated Knowledges: The Science Question in Feminism and the Privilege of Partial Perspective." *Feminist Studies*, vol. 14, no. 3, 1988, pp. 575-599.

Lara, Irene. "Sensing the Serpent in the Mother, Dando a Luz la Madre Serpiente: Chicana Spirituality, Sexuality, and Mamihood." *Fleshing the Spirit: Spirituality and Activism in Chicana, Latina, and Indigenous Women's Lives*, edited by Elisa Facio and Irene Lara, U of Arizona P, 2014, pp. 113–134.

---. "Healing Sueños for Academia." *this bridge we call home: radical visions for transformation*, edited by Gloria E. Anzaldúa and Analouise Keating, Routledge, 2002, pp. 433–438.

Moraga, Cherríe and Gloria Anzaldúa. "Entering the Lives of Others: Theory in the Flesh." *This Bridge Called my Back*, edited by Cherríe Moraga and Gloria Anzaldúa, 4th ed., State U of New York P, 2015, pp. 17–19.

# AUTOFANTASÍAS

## REINVENTING SELF & INSPIRING TRAVESURAS IN CHILDREN'S CULTURAL PRODUCTIONS

ISABEL MILLÁN

> I was the girl whose imagination swallowed the house, lagoon, corrals, and woods. My imagination made me pregnant with story. I literally ate my grandmothers' and mother's stories.
>
> —Gloria Anzaldúa (*Light in the Dark* 26)

Gloria Anzaldúa's vivacious imagination metamorphosed into canonical texts and transformative theories at the forefront of Chicana/o and queer of color scholarship. Much of her work extrapolates from her lived experience—stories regarding herself and those around her, such as her mother and grandmother. However, as a child, or queer Chicanita, she felt unseen and underrepresented in the stories she read throughout childhood. Thus, I want to begin with the assumption that queer Chicanx children often exist in isolation from each other, marginalized within their communities, or between multiple worlds.

While this may not be true for all queer Chicanx children, many, especially those of us unable to access others like us, are often made to believe we are odd or abnormal. We learn this as children, and if we are fortunate enough, we eventually find our niche, our communities. I am interested in facilitating this journey for queer Chicanx children who have not yet found their place within a collective home. These nepantleras lack materials that reflect or respond to their lived realities.

Gloria Anzaldúa made herself visible through her speaking, writing, illustrating, and teaching. She published two children's picture books and inspired many more. My examination of children's picture books prioritizes authors, illustrators, and creative thinkers who transform society through their oral and visual storytelling. Building on Gloria Anzaldúa's concept of autohistoria, I propose a theoretical and transformative tool, which I have termed autofantasía (Millán), that inspires travesuras within radical and unconventional children's cultural productions.

## CHILDHOOD TRAVESURAS AS AUTOFANTASÍAS

Reflecting on my childhood, I can now identify critical moments when I was socialized within heteronormativity, as well as moments I can now claim as my queer Chicana beginnings. Once while on the playground during recess, a boy insisted I not wear purple because it meant I was "gay." Although this occurred in the 1980s, his association of the color purple with queer identities was not entirely incorrect. The colors purple, violet, or lavender are associated with early gay and lesbian movements or organizations as well as the persecution of queer individuals identified through the "lavender scare" during McCarthyism and under former president Dwight D. Eisenhower (Johnson). While I may have not known then the definition of gay, much less its historical association with lavender, the tone in my classmate's voice made it clear he believed it was something repulsive I should shun. Unbeknownst to either of us at the time, I was already queer, even if I was only a child and even if I could not yet articulate it.

Part of the problem with one publicly coming out is that this act often negates all the queer moments that occurred prior to that public telling of our desires. For example, I vividly remember being in first grade and getting ready for picture day. I had short hair tucked to the side by a hairpiece and wore a white and pale pink cotton dress. My ensemble included a pair of Minnie Mouse earrings, which my mother purchased specifically for this occasion. The set also included a matching Minnie Mouse necklace. My mother looked forward to receiving my photographs, which were accompanied by headshots of the rest of my class along with headshots of the school's principal, vice principal, and my first-grade teacher. Within this class photograph, I was in the second row, fifth person from the left. To my mother's surprise, I was not wearing the necklace. I could have told her I lost it, but unfortunately for me, she quickly spotted the necklace on another one of my classmates—bottom row, third girl from the left. My mom was livid, repeatedly asking why one of my classmates was wearing my necklace. What I could not quite articulate at that moment was that she was not a random girl to me. I liked her more than just as a friend. I was taken by her smile and could not deny her request to borrow my necklace.

A few years later, I would develop a crush on another girl, this time the neighbor to the left of my childhood home. She was a couple of years older than me and I did everything possible to spend my time with her. She visited so often my mom began getting annoyed. I also remember playing with dolls and creating gay couplings among them, or dressing like what might be considered a tomboy, or being curious about one of my middle school teachers who was rumored to be gay. I share these moments or queer beginnings because they have shaped me into the queer Chicana I am today. And while I did eventually come out as a teenager, I wonder how my childhood might have been different had I known or learned about others like me.

What is the purpose of telling one's story? Of sharing our story with children? Or with our childhood selves? My childhood consisted of silence—literal silence imposed by my father. I was not allowed to speak. Meanwhile, I witnessed my father struggle with English and my mother battle with depression. Within my extended family, we have dealt with traumas ranging from mental health crises and cancer to sexual violence and suicides. How might my childhood have been different if I had felt whole? Heard? To answer these questions, I might imagine my current self having a conversation with my younger, child self, through autobiographically inspired children's picture books.

In 2015, I proposed autofantasía as a "literary technique whereby authors deliberately insert themselves within a text in order to fantasize solutions or responses to hegemonic structures" (202). This technique incorporates elements of autobiographic writing and fantasy fiction writing. It is also a reference to Gloria Anzaldúa's term autohistoria, which she defined as a retelling of one's past ("The New Mestiza Nation" 216; Keating 319). However, unlike autohistorias, autofantasías may represent a fictionalized past or an imagined future. By not restricting autofantasías to a specific time or place, authors and illustrators may move freely through space—recreating themselves within their works, such as in children's picture books, in order to propose solutions or counterhegemonic responses to socio-political problems.

Although I am privileging children's picture books, authors and illustrators may employ autofantasías within an array of media and genres. However, in my effort to prioritize unconventional or alternative works for children, the remainder of this essay focuses on queer Chicana author-activists. It is usually up to parents or caregivers to access alternative children's cultural productions. These may include, for example, children's picture books that center communities of color and queer families. Although there now exist classics such as Lesléa Newman's 1989 *Heather Has Two Mommies,*[1] or more independent and contemporary books such as Melissa Cardoza's 2004 *Tengo una tía que no es monjita [I Have an Aunt Who Is Not a Little Nun]*, these examples only depict queer adults. In order to prioritize queer children of color as an intended audience, I am drawn to authors and illustrators whose characters are also queer children of color. These include works from Gloria Anzaldúa as well as Maya Gonzalez, two queer Chicana artists, writers, and activists.

## GLORIA ANZALDÚA: QUEER CHICANA VISIONARY

Published posthumously in 2015, *Light in the Dark/Luz en lo oscuro: Rewriting Identity, Spirituality, Reality* became the latest rendition of Gloria Anzaldúa's writing and theorizing. Within it, she asks: "How real is reality?" (41). In response, she states: "To change or reinvent reality, you engage the facultad of your imagination" (44). "This conocimiento," she elaborates, "initiates the relationship between self-knowledge and creative work. Because the artist must keep watch on her inner responses, she becomes more aware, more alive, and thus she 'makes' the story of herself as she makes her art" (40). Anzaldúa was driven by an impulse, a desire, a sense of urgency to communicate and make meaning of her own reality through her writing. This impulse was, according to Anzaldúa, "a struggle to reconstruct oneself and heal the sustos resulting from woundings, traumas, racism, and other acts of violation que hechan pedazos nuestras almas, split us, scatter our energies, and haunt us" (1). She refers to this impulse as the Coyolxauhqui imperative. For Anzaldúa, then, creativity and storytelling were acts of healing and radical social change where "imagination opens the road to both personal and societal change—transformation of self, consciousness, community, culture, society (44).

Harriet Rohmer, publisher and founder of Children's Book Press, contacted Anzaldúa in 1988, roughly five years prior to the publication of her first children's picture book, *Friends from the Other Side/Amigos del otro lado* (1993). Rohmer's handwritten request went as follows:

> Dear Gloria,
>
> Good to hear from you. I hope all goes well in Santa Cruz.
> Here are Guidelines and Catalog. I'm also sending along a request we're sending to the community of Black writers here—for you to pass along...
> So, Gloria, perhaps you will send a Texas story soon. I hope so. I can't wait...
>
> Best,
> Harriet
>
> ("Letter to Gloria Anzaldúa" 1988)

This letter suggests their prior communication regarding a possible children's story set in Texas. Anzaldúa took the request seriously, writing an initial draft as early as March 15, 1989, and titling it "Prietita Makes a Friend" ("Handwritten draft of *Friends*"). Despite its early draft form, it already contained most of what would eventually become the characters and plot of *Friends*. Anzaldúa simultaneously enrolled in courses and workshops on children's literature, including a course by Lucille Clifton[2] at the University of California, Santa Cruz, and "New Dawn on the Horizon: Multicultural Experiences in Children's Literature," conducted in 1989 by Daphne Muse—then multicultural consultant, author, and executive editor of the *Children's Advocate Newspaper* (Anzaldúa "[Muse, D]"). This is not surprising, since, as AnaLouise Keating has noted, "Anzaldúa approached her writing like a ritual or a prayer. Her creative process was thoughtful, recursive, and communal, involving extensive research, multiple, heavily revised drafts, and peer critiques with her 'writing comadres' and others" (7). Anzaldúa confirms this in the acknowledgments section of her second children's book, stating, "I'd like to acknowledge and thank: Harriet Rohmer, who asked me to start writing for children; Lucille Cliffton, who introduced me to the craft in her class at UCSC; Lynda Marin, my comadre in writing who took the class with me; Francisco Alarcón, who enthusiastically read my cuentos; and David Schecter, for his insightful reading of my work" (*Prietita and the Ghost Woman*). *Friends* went through several revisions. By November of 1989, Anzaldúa had already typed and revised the narrative in both English and Spanish over six times, sharing several of these drafts with those around her.

In addition to her initial inspiration, collective writing process, and research into children's literature, Anzaldúa gradually became aware of the publishing industry's constraints for producing and distributing bilingual children's literature. Correspondence between Anzaldúa and editors Harriet Rohmer and David Schecter from Children's Book Press included great concern over the title of her second children's picture book, which was eventually published as *Prietita and the Ghost Woman/Prietita y la Llorona* (1995). One of the dilemmas entailed translating folklore figures and icons such as la Llorona. They eventually settled on "ghost woman," although they had also discussed using other possible translations, such as "spirit woman," or removing this figure from the title altogether. Anzaldúa was also keen on including Prietita's name within the picture book's title, although it was a Spanish nickname and had to petition the editors repeatedly. In one letter, dated August 14, 1995, titles ranged from "The Little Girl and the Ghost Woman" to "Lost in the woods" within a list of approximately eighteen suggestions (Anzaldúa, "Letter to Harriet Rohmer and David Schecter"). In another personal letter to Harriet Rohmer and David Schecter, dated August 22, 1995, Anzaldúa continues to express concern over the title: "I've been waking up worrying about the title, thinking up titles". She attaches a list with twenty-two additional suggested titles, some of which are translated into Spanish. She persists once again in a follow-up letter dated less than a week later. Referencing other Children's Book Press titles, Anzaldúa reminds Schecter and Rohmer that they have previously published "other 'foreign' sounding names" (see Figure 1).

She also discussed these frustrations in interviews, sharing that the State of Texas had the most conservative restrictions on children's curricula, limiting what publishers could include in picture books if they intended to circulate these within the public educational system (Anzaldúa "Toward a Mestiza Rhetoric" 259; Anzaldúa "Writing" 245). Most of what she was able to "get away with" ("Toward

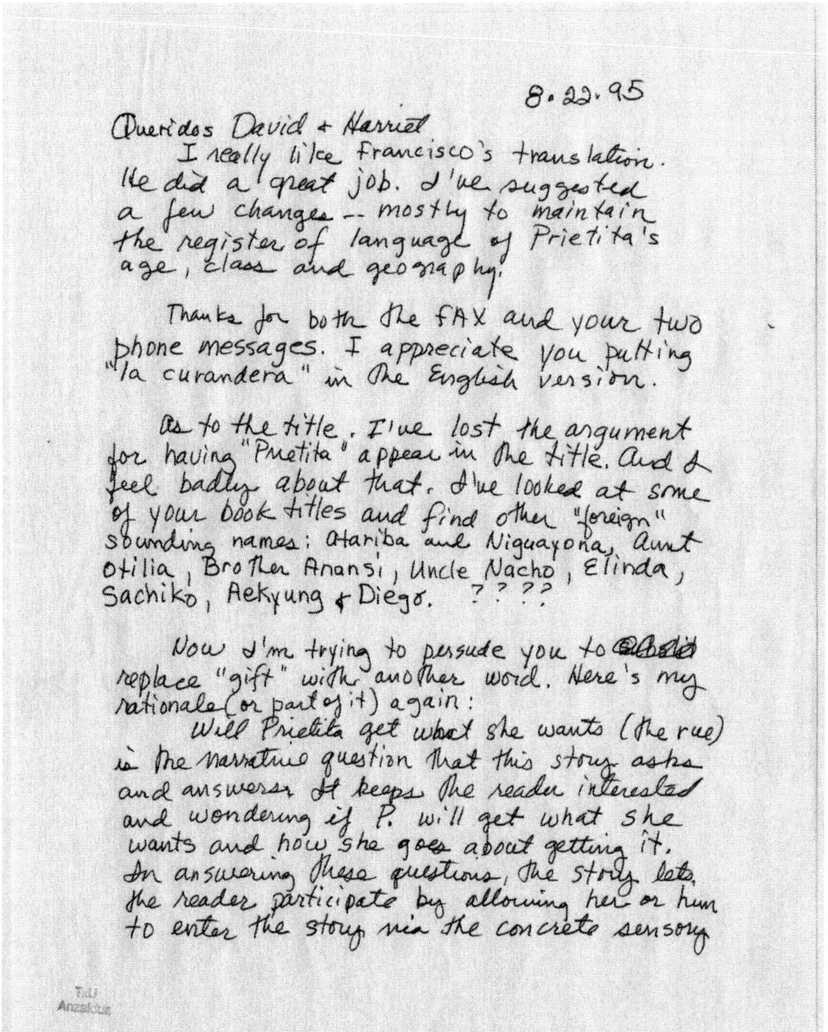

8.22.95

Queridos David + Harriet

I really like Francisco's translation. He did a great job. I've suggested a few changes -- mostly to maintain the register of language of Prietita's age, class and geography.

Thanks for both the FAX and your two phone messages. I appreciate you putting "la curandera" in the English version.

As to the title, I've lost the argument for having "Prietita" appear in the title. And I feel badly about that. I've looked at some of your book titles and find other "foreign" sounding names: Atariba and Niguayona, Aunt Otilia, Brother Anansi, Uncle Nacho, Elinda, Sachiko, Aekyung & Diego. ????

Now I'm trying to persude you to ~~[illegible]~~ replace "gift" with another word. Here's my rationale (or part of it) again:

Will Prietita get what she wants (the rue) is the narrative question that this story asks and answers. It keeps the reader interested and wondering if P. will get what she wants and how she goes about getting it. In answering these questions, the story lets the reader participate by allowing her or him to enter the story via the concrete sensory

TxU Anzaldúa

**Figure 1. 1995 Letter from Anzaldúa to David Schecter and Harriet Rohmer, pages 1 and 2. Anzaldúa Papers, 1942–2004, Nettie Benson Latin American Collection © The Gloria E. Anzaldúa Literary Trust. May not be reprinted without permission.**

a Mestiza Rhetoric" 259) dealt with immigration as well as language and translations as evidenced in her biography at the end of *Friends*, which read as follows:

> Gloria Anzaldúa is a major Mexican-American/Chicana literary voice. She is author of *Borderlands/La Frontera*, the editor of *Making Face, Making Soul*, and the co-editor of *This Bridge Called My Back: Writing by Radical Women of Color* (winner of the Before Columbus Foundation

Anzaldúa

(2)

images -- feel what P. is feeling, see what P. is seeing. P. is feeling tension, she's feeling lost and scared, she doesn't know if she'll find the herb or the way out. When the reader identifies with P and her feelings, she finds pleasure in discovering the answers as the story unravels. This pleasure is taken away when she is given too heavy a hint of the answer. Kids like to solve mysteries; they like riddles. The cover picture and "the ghost Woman's gift" give it all away. The title you are invested in using diminishes the suspense. It ~~tells who~~ that P gets the herb and it tells who helped her get it.

In the hope that you will change your mind at this, the 11th hour, I offer some other nouns (and gerunds) to go with ghost Woman (no apostrophes), words that go with the cover picture though that, again, is not one I'm enthralled with.

In the Presence of the Ghost Woman
The Presence of the Ghost Woman
Meeting the Ghost Woman
Encountering the Ghost Woman
The Ghost Woman Appears
The Apparition
~~El~~ A Dark Woman [Dressed] In White
The Ghost Woman
The Moon Moved in The Sky

keeping my fingers crossed that you'll change your mind. Contigo, Gloria

TxU Anzaldúa

**Figure 1 cont.**

> American Book Award). The Spanish that she uses in this story is the Chicano Spanish spoken by many Mexican American people and is different from the Spanish used in Latin America and Spain. (n.p.)

Evidently, Anzaldúa was restricted to the publishing guidelines set in order to bypass potential censorship. In part, this was due to the publisher's target audience and their desire to circulate *Friends* within public elementary schools across the US.

To Anzaldúa's surprise, another unlikely audience sprung from within academia and college settings. In a note to Laura Atkins she describes her experience on college campuses: "I just returned from two gigs where the campus bookstores were selling *Amigos del otro lado* like hot cakes. They lined up for hours during my autograph sessions." ("Letter/fax to Laura Atkins"). On a separate occasion she writes: "This book is taught in college courses—can you believe that? It's taught in children's literature courses. Professors buy it for their kids or nietos or sobrinos or for themselves! So it's for both adults and children" (Anzaldúa "Writing" 245). Like state regulations or industry standards, unintended audiences, such as those within academia, may also contribute to the production, distribution, and consumption of these books.

Though US-based, *Friends* materialized as a transnational project further regulated by the nonprofit status of Children's Book Press. On the mass production and distribution front, *Friends* was printed in Hong Kong by Marwin Productions, and was published under the project "Books About You and Me"—financially supported by the California Arts Council, the Wallace Alexander Gerbode Foundation, the Fleishhacker Foundation, the Wells Fargo Foundation, the Neutrogena Corporation, and the Morris Stulsaft Foundation (Anzaldúa, *Friends*). This donor's list is indicative of the growing interest by major corporations in children's literature. We might ponder what they have to gain from their financial sponsorship, or how their financial contributions may also influence the actual content of these books.

A children's picture book is made up of not only the text or story, but also of illustrations. *Friends* was illustrated by Venezuelan painter and graphic artist Consuelo Méndez, who began sketches while in Houston, Texas, and completed the final illustrations from Caracas, Venezuela (Méndez).[3] The author and illustrator's shared background of Texas is mentioned in a Press Release of *Friends* by the Children's Book Press dated January 6, 1993: "Both Gloria Anzaldúa and Consuelo Méndez grew up near the US-Mexico border. In this, their first collaboration, they have captured the beauty of the landscape as well as the dignity and generosity of spirit that the Mexican Americans and the Mexican immigrants share" (Children's Book Press). While they each grew up within a similar geographic location, Méndez is not Chicana—challenging the assumption that all Latinx communities on the US-Mexico border are Mexican or Chicanx. Within her biography, she is described as "a painter and graphic artist from Caracas, Venezuela, whose work is widely exhibited in Latin America" (Children's Book Press). It continues, "She spent a large part of her growing up years in South Texas before coming to San Francisco to study art. She returned to South Texas in order to do research for this book, which she illustrated in watercolors, graphite and colored pencils and collage" (Children's Book Press).

Although the illustrations in *Friends* are shaped by both the author's and illustrator's background and knowledge of South Texas, the narrative is most indicative of Anzaldúa's implementation of autofantasía. She writes herself into the story through the child protagonist, Prietita. This name is not surprising, given Anzaldúa's 1981 essay "La Prieta" in *This Bridge Called My Back: Writings by*

*Radical Women of Color*. She described in detail how her skin tone and phenotype were perceived within her own family, including by her grandmother: "Too bad mihijita [*sic*] was morena, *muy prieta*, so dark and different from her own fair-skinned children. But she loved mihijita anyway. What I lacked in whiteness, I had in smartness. But it *was* too bad I was dark like an Indian" (Anzaldúa "La Prieta" 198, italics in original).

Within *Friends*, Anzaldúa once again reclaims the nickname Prietita, this time in the context of a fictionalized setting and as a queer Chicanita who befriends Joaquín, an undocumented boy from Mexico. Within this picture book, Anzaldúa recreates herself as a child and a heroine through the character of Prietita. As such, she protects Joaquin from neighborhood bullies, attempts to secure him work, and hides him and his mother from border patrol agents.[4] A secondary character, la curandera, also plays a critical role in *Friends*—constructed as healer and protector. Both Prietita and la curandera reappear in Anzaldúa's second children's picture book. However, this time, Anzaldúa also reimagines herself as a healer by taking on the role of the curandera's apprentice while on a search for herbs to help heal her mother.

Tragically, Anzaldúa's own health complications with diabetes resulted in her death in 2004. Her legacy lives on not only within Prietita, but also through the ongoing dedication of the Society for the Study of Gloria Anzaldúa (SSGA) as well as practitioners of Anzaldúa studies and borderlands theory.

## MAYA GONZALEZ, FROM FINE ARTIST TO AUTHOR/ILLUSTRATOR

Anzaldúa inspired, and continues to inspire, artists-activists such as Maya Gonzalez, a queer Chicana artist, illustrator, and author, currently living in San Francisco, California. She is primarily known for her vibrant and provocative paintings, which have graced the covers of novels, monographs, and anthologies such as Carla Trujillo's edited volume *Living Chicana Theory* (1998), and tatiana de la tierra's collection *For the Hard Ones: A Lesbian Phenomenology/Para las duras: Una fenomenología lesbiana* (2002) as well as for her children's book illustrations such as *Prietita and the Ghost Woman*, previously mentioned. Her collaboration with Anzaldúa shifted her focus toward children's picture books, illustrating numerous others for Children's Book Press. These included books by Francisco X. Alarcón, such as *Laughing Tomatoes and Other Spring Poems/Jitomates Risueños y otros poemas de primavera* (1997) and *From the Bellybutton of the Moon and Other Summer Poems/Del Ombligo de la Luna y otros poemas de verano* (1998), as well as books by Amada Irma Pérez, such as *My Very Own Room/Mi propio cuartito* (2000) and *My Diary from Here to There/Mi diario de aquí hasta allá* (2002). As a children's book illustrator, she learned industry standards along the way while also discovering the transformative potential of picture books (Gonzalez, "Personal Interview").

Gonzalez's more recent works for children are children's picture books that she both illustrated and authored. These include *My Colors, My World/Mis colores, mi mundo* (2007), and *I Know the River Loves Me/Yo sé que el río me ama* (2009), both of which were published by Children's Book Press. Like Anzaldúa, Gonzalez creates autofantasías whereby she inserts herself into her children's picture books—and in the case of *Colors* and *River*, she inserts herself as the child protagonist. Her use of autofantasía takes readers first through a world of colors as she describes her childhood home and, secondly, through a love letter or poem describing her affinity with rivers. She writes in the first person, allowing her audience to feel as if she is directly speaking to us. Gonzalez begins, "I am here to visit one of my best friends in the world, the river. She loves me. I know the river loves me because I can hear her calling me as soon as I am close" (*River* 2–4). Although the protagonist's name is never mentioned, for those of us familiar with Gonzalez and her artwork, we can identify aspects of Gonzalez in both the text and illustrations. Additionally, Gonzalez's biography at the end of the book begins with "Maya Christina Gonzalez is a river lover" (24). This page includes two photographs of herself next to rivers; her hair is split in two and tied up, like that of her character, which she has also drawn with a similar chin, mole, and ear piercings resembling her own (see Figure 2).

**Figure 2. Cover of *I Know the River Loves Me/Yo sé que el río me ama* © Maya Christina Gonzalez.**

This illustrated version of herself makes regular appearances throughout Gonzalez's other autofantasías for children, including *Gender Now Coloring Book: A Learning Adventure for Children and Adults*, self-published in 2010 through Reflection Press. The cover reads: "I am Free to Be Me!" At the bottom, Gonzalez depicts six children whose t-shirts collectively spell out "G-E-N-D-E-R." She inserts herself as one of the characters, the letter R at the end. Gonzalez dedicates the coloring book to her child, Zai, whom she describes as "free": "You are beautiful free. May all your days be filled with this knowing" (*Gender Now* n.p.). Page one begins with a direct address to "parents, caregivers, therapists, social workers, teachers and all the fabulous grown-ups sharing a gender exploration/adventure with children," suggesting adults read it first before sharing it with students in order to familiarize themselves with the content. "This book is just a beginning," states Gonzalez, and its primary goal after sharing basic knowledge on gender is to "support and inspire each of us to be exactly who we are" (1).

Gonzalez is deliberate in her use of "we." She has inserted herself within this coloring book not only as author and illustrator, but also as one of the children. Specifically, she is now an adult who has recreated herself into a child within an autofantasía, or queer-inclusive world, which was not necessarily her own in real life. In her biography at the end, she shares how she came out at the age of twenty and was rejected by her family, and shares the importance of finding adequate books to educate and celebrate her daughter as well as acknowledge her queer family and trans partner, Matthew Smith-Gonzalez.

One of the coloring book activities includes matching three children to their respective nude bodies and then matching these to their respective preferred play activities. Gonzalez deliberately plays on gender stereotypes by pairing the child who might be read as female or a girl with the toolset including a hammer and nails. She then juxtaposes this child with another one who might be read as male or a boy with the teddy bear and sewing kit. Another activity states: "Color us however you want. You can even dress us in whatever clothes you imagine" (*Gender Now* 12). Like the other nude bodies, Gonzalez is using an illustrated version of her child self in order for her audience to engage in discussions around gender and bodies.

Although Gonzalez's earlier works were published with notable mainstream presses such as Children's Books Press, now an imprint of Lee and Low Books Inc.,[5] the limits imposed by the children's book industry led her to create Reflection Press, an independent book press, along with the School of the Free Mind, where she shares her skills and mentors aspiring authors and artists. Reflection Press' mission is to "provide materials that support a strong sense of individuality along with a community model of real inclusion" ("Our Mission & Values"). Its vision is to "envision a world rooted in true freedom, respect, and equality, and motivated by the knowledge that everyone is valuable and everyone has special creative gifts to share" ("Our Mission & Values").

Gonzalez's curriculum is guided by three rules: (1) Everyone is an Artist, (2) There is never a right or wrong way to make art, and (3) Art is always an act of courage (*Maya Gonzalez*). These rules apply to both adults and children, having worked with all age demographics. She utilizes her "Write Now! Make Books" curriculum with children in classrooms. Reflecting on these experiences in an interview with Lisa Dettmer, Gonzalez states,

> when I would go into the classrooms what I realized was that…it's not about teaching them to draw a face, it's just teaching them to be very present for a moment with me and giving them the tools that art was some way that they could also be very present with themselves.

She goes on, "It didn't matter what it looked like at the end of the day…it could look hideous" ("Why I Create Children's Books"). By emphasizing art as a tool as opposed to a technique, Gonzalez is prioritizing her ability to empower children through a sense of self-awareness, or as she states, "a kind of presence with themselves and also a consciousness where they could express things that didn't have words" ("Why I Create Children's Books"). For example, each child might create something that more closely reflects or communicates their prior experiences, joys, traumas, or connections to others without necessarily being legible to others.

While Reflection Press allows Gonzalez the freedom to create and distribute books, reading guides, and curricula outside of the traditional or mainstream children's book industry, her online school, SFM (School of the Free Mind), provides direct mentorship and guidance for aspiring children's book authors and illustrators or anyone else who might be interested in alternative pedagogies and radical cultural productions. In addition to mentoring aspiring children's book authors, she showcases excerpts of their work in three edited volumes published by Reflection Press: *Whale Heart: The Heart of It Anthology #1* (2015), *By the Light of the Rabbit Moon: The Heart of It Anthology #2* (2016), and *Unfurling: Voice is a Revolution Anthology #3* (2017) in an effort to launch more independent children's cultural productions. In *Whale Heart* she writes,

> It's important to see ourselves in the world around us. When I was a little girl I didn't see faces or experiences or art or words like mine in my books or anywhere. I remember drawing my round Chicana face into the backs of books. I must have noticed that I was missing and imagined that I belonged there. What I know now is that if we don't find books that reflect us, we can make our own! We don't have to keep looking or draw ourselves in. We can make our own books and we can begin right now.[6]

Through this experience, each aspiring author or illustrator gains visibility as well as valuable experience in crafting a two-page spread, which may stand on its own or be an excerpt of a larger, ongoing project.

Like Gloria Anzaldúa, Maya Gonzalez saw the transformative power of children's picture books while also experiencing the limitations and pressures imposed by the children's book industry and the public education system. Motivated by a sense of urgency exacerbated by today's political climate, Gonzalez further aims to inspire marginalized individuals and communities to tell their own stories through children's picture books. In 2016, she created an Indiegogo fundraising campaign titled *Children's Books as a Radical Act*, meant to fund the creation of six additional children's picture books that center "people of color, indigenous, and queer voices and experiences" ("Children's Books as a Radical Act"). And, in 2017, in response to the latest US presidential election, Gonzalez wrote and illustrated *When a Bully is President: Truth and Creativity for Oppressive Times/Cuando el president es un bulí: La verdad y la creatividad en tiempos opresivos*. Describing it as "not your usual kid's book," she deliberately published it through her independent press in order to craft it precisely as she intended—as a social justice tool meant to "push the limits of what's possible in publishing" (*When a Bully is President* 2). Gonzalez's repertoire continues to grow as she self-publishes more recent titles such as a young adult novel, *Ma Llorona:*

*A Ghost Story, A Love Story* (2017), a coloring book, *Coloring the Revolution #1* (2017), and other children's picture books, including *The Gender Wheel: A Story About Bodies and Gender for Every Body* (2017) and *They She He Me: Free to Be!* (2017), which she co-wrote with her partner Matthew Smith-Gonzalez.

## CREATING CHABELITA, CREATING SELF

Both Gloria Anzaldúa and Maya Gonzalez inspired those around them to create, to share themselves with the world, to tell their stories. They each accomplished this through children's picture books by deliberately inserting themselves within the text and illustrations of their works. Utilizing autofantasía as a literary and aesthetic technique, they recreated their childhoods in order to comment on themes and socio-political issues outside of what is usually considered appropriate content for children.

Inspired by Anzaldúa and Gonzalez, I, too, have stories I want to share in the form of a children's picture book. Growing up, my family and friends called me María, Mari, and Marilou, or Chabelita and Isabela for Isabel. Just like I had many nicknames, I reimagine myself in many forms as I draft and sketch my own autofantasías. Sometimes my illustrations look like variations of me, while other times, there is no apparent resemblance. As I write and sketch the initial draft of my forthcoming children's picture book, I am reminded of everyone who has touched my life and of the future generations of queer children of color who will continue to struggle for visibility, representation, autonomy, and a more just world.

I consider decolonial love as an action-oriented process of healing from the collective traumas of colonization. Our understanding of histories and politics are interlinked with the corporeal, the visceral, the emotional, the psychological, and the unknown. Communities include everyone from our elders to our children, all of whom are vital to our collective survival. Gloria Anzaldúa reminds us to move forward "con la lengua en la mano izquierda" and, after a screening of these words during El Mundo Zurdo 2016, Rita E. Urquijo-Ruiz added, con "el corazón."[7] Thus, "con la lengua y el corazón en la mano izquierda," may we all share pieces of ourselves, whether it be through autohistorias or autofantasías in order to not just theorize our existence, but enact and reenact it through the multiple processes of praxis.

## NOTES

1. Lesléa Newman first independently co-published *Heather Has Two Mommies* in 1989 with Tzivia Gover under In Other Words Publishing. It was initially illustrated by Diana Souza. Newman then published the picture book with Alyson Wonderland. A more recent rendition was illustrated by Laura Cornell and published by Candlewick Press in 2015. For a discussion of *Heather Has Two Mommies*'s publishing history and its multiple editions, see Hetter, Kellogg.

2. Lucille Clifton conducted these courses between 1985 and 1989. It is unclear when Anzaldúa enrolled.

3. Carmen Lomas Garza originally agreed to illustrate *Friends*. It is unclear from the archival record how the transition from Garza to Méndez occurred. For more context, see the exchange between Anzaldúa and Rohmer.

4. For a close reading of *Friends*, see Millán 207-14.

5. Harriet Rohmer began Children's Book Press in 1975 with a grant from the US Department of Education (see https://www.leeandlow.com/imprints/children-s-book-press/articles/children-s-book-press-history). However, it became an imprint of Lee and Low Books Inc. in 2012 (see Werris).

6. Although this is not a picture book, the anthology does not include page numbers. This description appears toward the end of the collection, between the main story and "Meet the Storytellers."

7. During El Mundo Zurdo 2016's Welcome Reception at The Esperanza in San Antonio, Texas, the conference organizers screened footage of Gloria Anzaldúa delivering a previous talk.

## WORKS CITED

Alarcón, Francisco X. *From the Bellybutton of the Moon and Other Summer Poems/Del Ombligo de la Luna y otros poemas de verano.* Illustrated by Maya Christina Gonzalez. Children's Book Press, 1998.

---. *Laughing Tomatoes and Other Spring Poems/Jitomates Risueños y otros poemas de primavera.* Illustrated by Maya Christina Gonzalez. Children's Book Press, 1997.

Anzaldúa, Gloria. *Borderlands/La Frontera: The New Mestiza.* Aunt Lute, 1987.

---. *Friends from the Other Side/Amigos del otro lado.* Illustrated by Consuelo Méndez. Children's Book Press, 1993.

---. Handwritten draft of *Friends.* 15 March 1988. Gloria Evangelina Anzaldúa Papers, Benson Latin American Collection, University of Texas at Austin. Box 71, folder 10.

---. Letter to Harriet Rohmer and David Schecter. 14 August 1995. Gloria Evangelina Anzaldúa Papers. Benson Latin American Collection, University of Texas at Austin. Box 9, folder 4.

---. Letter to Harriet Rohmer and David Schecter. 22 August 1995. Gloria Evangelina Anzaldúa Papers. Benson Latin American Collection, University of Texas at Austin. Box 75, folder 19.

---. Letter/fax to Laura Atkins. 10 October 1995. Gloria Evangelina Anzaldúa Papers. Benson Latin American Collection, University of Texas at Austin. Box 9, folder 4.

---. *Light in the Dark/Luz en lo Oscuro: Rewriting Identity, Spirituality, Reality.* Edited by AnaLouise Keating, Duke UP, 2015.

---. [Muse, D]. handouts. Circa. 1989. Gloria Evangelina Anzaldúa Papers. Benson Latin American Collection, University of Texas at Austin. Box 71, folder 9.

---. "The New Mestiza Nation: A Multicultural Movement." *The Gloria Anzaldúa Reader,* edited by AnaLouise Keating, Duke UP, 2009, pp. 203–16.

---. "La Prieta." *This Bridge Called My Back,* edited by Gloria Anzaldúa and Cherríe Moraga, Persephone Press, 1981, pp. 198–209.

---. *Prietita and the Ghost Woman/Prietita y la Llorona.* Illustrated by Maya Christina Gonzalez. Children's Book Press, 1995.

---. "Toward a Mestiza Rhetoric: Gloria Anzaldúa on Composition, Postcoloniality, and the Spiritual." *Interviews/Entrevistas,* edited by AnaLouise Keating, Routledge, 2000, pp. 251–80.

---. "Writing: A Way of Life. An Interview with María Henríquez Betancor." *Interviews/Entrevistas,* edited by AnaLouise Keating, Routledge, 2000, pp. 235–50.

Cardoza, Melissa. *Tengo una tía que no es monjita.* Illustrated by Margarita Sada. Patlatonalli, 2004.

Children's Book Press. Press Release for *Friends From the Other Side.* 6 January 1993. Gloria Evangelina Anzaldúa Papers. Benson Latin American Collection, University of Texas at Austin. Box 9, folder 4.

de la tierra, tatiana. *For the Hard Ones: A Lesbian Phenomenology/Para las duras: Una fenomenología lesbiana.* Calaca Press, 2002.

---. *Xia y las mil sirenas.* Illustrated by Anna Cooke. Patlatonalli, 2009.

Gonzalez, Maya Christina. *By the Light of the Rabbit Moon: The Heart of It Anthology #2*. Reflection Press, 2016.

---. *Call Me Tree/Llámame* árbol. Children's Book Press, 2014.

---. "Children's Books as a Radical Act." Indiegogo. https://www.indiegogo.com/projects/children-s-books-as-a-radical-act#/ Accessed 14 June 2017.

---. *Coloring the Revolution #1*. Press, 2017.

---. *Gender Now Coloring Book: A Learning Adventure for Children and Adults*. Reflection Press, 2010.

---. *The Gender Wheel: A Story About Bodies and Gender for Every Body.* Reflection Press, 2017.

---. *I Know the River Loves Me/Yo sé que el río me ama.* Children's Book Press, 2009.

---. *Ma Llorona: A Ghost Story, A Love Story.* Reflection Press, 2017.

---. *Maya Gonzalez: Artist, Author, Educator, Activist*. http://www.mayagonzalez.com/. Accessed 14 June 2017.

---. *My Colors, My World/Mis colores, mi mundo*. Children's Book Press, 2007.

---. Personal Interview. 21 October 2016.

---. *Unfurling: Voice is a Revolution Anthology #3*. Reflection Press, 2017.

---. *Whale Heart: The Heart of It Anthology #1*. Reflection Press, 2015.

---. *When a Bully is President: Truth and Creativity for Oppressive Times/Cuando el president es un bulí: La verdad y la creatividad en tiempos opresivos*. Reflection Press, 2017.

---. "Why I Create Children's Books." *Maya Gonzalez: Artist, Author, Educator, Activist*. http://www.mayagonzalez.com/. Accessed 14 June 2017.

Gonzalez, Maya Christina, and Matthew Smith-Gonzalez. *They She He Me: Free to Be!* Reflection Press, 2017.

Hetter, Katia. "'Heather Has Two Mommies' Comes Out Again." *CNN.com*, 24 March 2015, http://www.cnn.com/2015/03/24/living/feat-heather-has-two-mommies-lesleanewman/index.html. Accessed 7 October 2017.

Johnson, David K. *The Lavender Scare: The Cold War Persecution of Gays and Lesbians in the Federal Government*. U of Chicago P, 2004.

Keating, AnaLouise, editor. *The Gloria Anzaldúa Reader.* Duke UP, 2009.

Kellogg, Carolyn. "Once Controversial, 'Heather Has Two Mommies' is Now Collectible." *LATimes.com*, 11 May 2017, http://www.latimes.com/books/jacketcopy/la-ca-jc-heather-has-two-mommies-20170511-story.html. Accessed 6 October 2017.

Méndez, Consuelo. Letters to Gloria Anzaldúa. 13 September 1991 and 10 June 1992. Gloria Evangelina Anzaldúa Papers. Benson Latin American Collection, University of Texas at Austin. Box 71, folder 7.

Millán, Isabel. "Contested Children's Literature: Que(e)ries into Chicana and Central American *Autofantasías*." *Signs: Journal of Women in Culture and* Society, vol. 41, no. 1, 2015, pp. 199–224. https://doi.org/10.1086/681919.

Newman, Lesléa. *Heather has Two Mommies*. Illustrated by Diana Souza. Alyson Wonderland, 1989.

"Our Mission & Values." *Reflections Press*, http://www.reflectionpress.com/about-us/mission-values/. Accessed 14 June 2017.

Pérez, Amada Irma. *My Diary from Here to There/Mi diario de aquí hasta allá*. Illustrated by Maya Christina Gonzalez. Children's Book Press, 2002.

---. *My Very Own Room/Mi propio cuartito*. Illustrated by Maya Christina Gonzalez. Children's Book Press, 2000.

Rohmer, Harriet. Letter to Gloria Anzaldúa. 4 August 1988, Gloria Evangelina Anzaldúa Papers. Benson Latin American Collection, University of Texas at Austin, TX. Box 71, folder 8.

---. Letter to Gloria Anzaldúa. 21 February 1990. Gloria Evangelina Anzaldúa Papers. Benson Latin American Collection, University of Texas at Austin. Box 71, folder 8.

Trujillo, Carla, editor. *Living Chicana Theory*. Third Woman Press, 1998.

Werris, Wendy. "Lee & Low Acquires Children's Book Press." *Publishersweekly.com*, 26 Jan 2012, https://www.publishersweekly.com/pw/by-topic/childrens/childrens-industry-news/article/50362-lee-low-acquires-children-s-book-press.html. Accessed 1 October 2017.

# 'A COUNTRY I INVENTED'

## CURATING AN ANZALDÚAN SPIRITUALITY AND ANTI-NEOLIBERAL NARRATIVE IN SANDRA CISNEROS'S *CARAMELO*

JENNIFER LOZANO

Anyone fortunate enough to visit the Gloria E. Anzaldúa papers housed in the Nettie Lee Benson Latin American Collection at the University of Texas at Austin can likely attest to the cognitive and material excesses of its 200-plus boxes of archival material. Beyond the perhaps typical opacity of scholarly archives, the Anzaldúa papers are extra confounding because of the sheer borderlessness of their content. To name just a few inclusions, Anzaldúa scholars will sift through writing notes scribbled on the back of doctor's appointment reminders; receipts—and notes on the receipts—from speaking gigs; various spiritual texts and prayer cards; and countless essay revisions with handwritten commentary and Post-it notes.[1] Despite the well-organized and highly controlled environment of the Benson Library, it is fruitless to try to sort out Anzaldúa's intellectual or creative output from her own bodily, spiritual, financial, and personal life experiences. This, of course, is not inconsistent with Anzaldúa's life work, which broke multiple conventions of scholarly writing and thought. In her final creative act, Anzaldúa thus reiterates the performative quality of her writing and its shamanistic ability—or, perhaps, imperative—to "transform the storyteller and the listener into something or someone else…" (*Borderlands* 88). As Suzanne Bost explains, rather than looking to Anzaldúa's archive to confirm or reject what we know about her, "the process of authority is…continued into the present and future, into the work done in the reading room and beyond" (622). Anzaldúa's work and archive intentionally involve the reader—physically, spiritually, and intellectually—in the process of interpretation and knowledge creation. This essay explores a similar practice in Sandra Cisneros's 2002 novel *Caramelo* that builds especially on Anzaldúa's concept of spiritual activism. In identifying this strategy, I contend that the narrative in *Caramelo* elaborates the powerful and pleasurable ability of female storytelling to map the felt experience of living in the borderlands as a diasporic Mexican/American subject. Moreover, by articulating the expansive scope and power of storytelling to historic, material, economic, and spiritual realms, Cisneros's spiritual activism revalues the work of Mexican/American literature and culture in a neoliberal social and political context that primarily values information and transactional exchange.[2] To the contrary, the novel's voluminous and intertextual storytelling resist this type of interpretation.

## NEOLIBERALISM AND LITERARY CULTURE

Despite its seeming ubiquity in academic conversations about the university and other (shrinking) public services, the term "neoliberalism" still tends to be a buzzword that, too often, goes unexplained. According to David Harvey, the theory of neoliberalism can be traced back to 1979 and to the statecraft of then–US Federal Reserve leader Paul Volker and British Prime Minister Margaret Thatcher, who managed to revive a minoritarian economic doctrine and transform it into the dominant principle of economic management (2). This economic theory, however, is distinctive in that it also extends into the social and political organization of society. As Harvey explains: "Neoliberalism is...a theory of political economic practices that proposes that human well-being can best be advanced by liberating individual entrepreneurial freedoms and skills within an institutional framework characterized by strong private property rights, free markets, and free trade" (2). In this way, while the more all-encompassing and obfuscating term "globalization" can be understood as the expansion of capitalism into ever larger and international realms, neoliberalism refers to the "new rules of functioning of capitalism" (Duménil and Levy qtd. in Dowdy 8). In its role as the dominant interpretive framework for global capital, then, neoliberalism has also captured a significant portion of our contemporary imagination for human, social, and cultural potential and well-being. In other words, neoliberalism has significantly influenced the discourse of value and even of philosophical belief in the US.

The degree to which neoliberalism has impacted Latina/o cultural production and interpretation, however, is not a frequent topic of scholarly discussion. Most notably, scholars such as George Yúdice and Arlene Dávila have made important contributions to our understanding of the effects of globalization and neoliberalism on the production, circulation, and reception of culture. With regard to specifically literary cultural production, there are even fewer studies that focus on the cultural impact of neoliberalism (Dowdy 8).[3] Among these, Jodi Melamed's 2011 *Represent and Destroy: Rationalizing Violence in the New Racial Capitalism* stands out for its comprehensive approach to studying the institutionalization of minority literary culture and the co-opting role of the state and capital in its production, circulation, and reception.[4] Particularly, in her assessment of "neoliberal multiculturalism," Melamed documents the neoliberal demand to read minority literature (now often called "global literature") from the perspective of the privileged global citizen and with the aim to provide simplistic information about a "foreign" culture, to facilitate connection with "good" minorities and an explanation of "bad" minorities, as well as to facilitate the self-care of elites vis-à-vis the notion that diverse literature provides readers with anti-racist moral value (158–161). Melamed also identifies and reads some literary texts as "race radical" and in defiance of these co-opting tendencies. *Represent and Destroy* provides rich and diverse evidence for its thesis, but one reductive effect of the study is its creation and maintenance of a binary between "good" or politically viable and "bad" or politically unviable literature that may elide the complex dynamics of neoliberalism and culture. To the contrary, a spiritually active writing and interpretive practice does not emphasize a clearly legible "good" or politically viable cultural representation, but seeks to foreground and uncover complex (often excessive) experiences of nation, race, gender, ethnicity, sexuality, and class in creative ways that bypass a solely identity-based cultural politics. As we will see in Cisneros, this practice can also foreground a certain pleasure of female storytelling that both articulates a sense of place in displacement and eschews dominant neoliberal interpretive values.

## ANZALDÚA'S SPIRITUAL ACTIVISM

While Anzaldúa's emphasis on spirituality and her concept of spiritual activism are important components of a larger women-of-color feminist tradition, it is important to return to her own writing and its insistence on spirituality as necessary for queer, radical visioning (Delgadillo 13–14).[5] From her earliest published work, but increasingly in her later work, Anzaldúa maintained a keen and revisionist sense of the political importance of spirituality, especially for multiply oppressed queer Chicana and Latina subjects. Arguably, one of Anzaldúa's most significant contributions to queer theory and queer world-making is her understanding of spirituality as deeply intertwined with the body, the physical and natural world, and our relationship with others and the environment or our social realm. These interconnections can be seen in *Borderlands/La Frontera* (1987) through her discussion of writing in "Tlilli, Tlapalli / The Path of the Red and Black Ink," her incorporation of Mesoamerican religion into theorizing her own identity and role in a collective culture, and even in her concept of a borderlands and a mestiza consciousness. Moreover, as scholars have recently explained, her interest in the political significance of a spiritual writing and lived practice is the most consistent and overlooked theme in her work (Keating "Citizen").

Never settling on a term to describe her spirituality, Anzaldúa used at least two terms to explicitly describe this aspect of her life: "spiritual mestizaje" and "spiritual activism." Spiritual mestizaje refers to her mixed blood embodiment as a mestiza, as well as the mix of different cultures, religions, and viewpoints that she inherits or self-consciously engages and that are fundamental to transforming her own identity as a queer Chicana feminist and for producing knowledge about the world (*Borderlands* 239). Studying Anzaldúa's work on the concept, Theresa Delgadillo notes that in *Borderlands* the author "works her own experience of spiritual, social, emotional, and intellectual journeying to theorize the significance of the U.S.-Mexico border in the creation and potential for the Chicana subject, particularly the queer Chicana subject" (1). Anzaldúa's idea of spirituality is also elaborated in her unpublished 1999 manuscript "Spiritual Activism: Making Altares, Making Connections," which is a part of her collected archive (box 64, folder 20). In this text, Anzaldúa reiterates the significance of both an embodied mestizaje or the "syncretism of different bloodlines" and a self-fashioned, socio-political mestizaje to her concept of spirituality. By insisting that spiritual mestizaje is a practice that involves both bloodlines and socio-political choices, Anzaldúa draws attention to the fact that cultural and spiritual practices are not divorced from ethnic, racialized, and sexed bodies. It is from an embodied experience that Anzaldúa's spiritual mestizaje begins. As she explains, for her, "la Virgen de Guadalupe is one of the central [spiritual] figures, one charged with significance" and this symbology evolves from her own memory of the framed picture of "la Virgencita" that her grandmother kept on her makeshift dresser top altar. Part of Anzaldúa's "spiritual history," as she puts it, is a "tradition of strong, enduring women" ("Spiritual Activism" 1–2). Spiritual mestizaje takes into account an embodied and historical experience even as it draws from other traditions and beliefs.

In this context, Anzaldúa's term spiritual activism becomes more vivid and apropos. Using the term "activism" highlights the way spirituality emerges from and is practiced through the body in a very political way. In Anzaldúa's words:

> When you become a spiritually active person, one who treats spiritual work as a political issue and who does outer- as well as innerwork, you start conceiving, or reconfiguring, the different component of reality in a different way. ... By expanding your 'take' of reality, you make connections, not only to the physical, psychological and spiritual worlds, but also to political realities ("Spiritual Activism" 2–3).

Here, inner and outer spiritual work can lead to altered perceptions of political realities and narrative strategies, as well as the spiritual energy needed to do this political work. Thus, for writers and artists, spiritual activism can work as a personal and imaginative resource that may or may not intersect with mainline, orthodox religion or doctrine. In fact, encountering the spiritual in *Caramelo* does not promote an orthodox or "right" way to be (e.g. resistant/unresistant, moral/immoral) a transnational Mexican/American subject so much as a dynamic way of being that is active, creative, cognizant, and relational. The confrontations and narrative excesses created by *Caramelo* are not the desired outcome, but are intended to instigate other social, material, intellectual and spiritual connections. Moreover, it is through the text's engagement with a flexible spirituality that the narratives attempt to queerly narrate and map diasporic Mexican/American lives, experiences, and expressions at a moment when valuation systems of the nation state, the market, and mainstream religion have proven unsatisfactory.

## STORYTELLING, TRANSNATIONAL CRITIQUES, AND NEOLIBERALISM IN *CARAMELO*

*Caramelo*, above all, is a novel about telling stories. A novel full of half-truths and melodrama, the stories primarily concern the adolescent narrator, Celaya, her transnational Mexican/American family, and a mounting tension with the Mexican grandmother who is also referred to by the protagonist as "the awful grandmother." A sense of embodied storytelling is quickly conveyed in the novel through its narrative structures. The novel is broken into eighty-six episodic vignettes largely narrated by Celaya, but also interspersed with interjections from the deceased "awful grandmother" who struggles for control from the beyond in parts II and III. Footnotes also add to the text's narrative form and accommodate its plentiful cultural and historical references. The result of these devices is the sense of a permanently present temporality or an ongoing performance given by a physically present narrator. As Amara Graf suggests, the novel reads as if the story is being told to a physical audience (4). At the same time, although the episodic quality and dueling narrators offer physicality and immediacy to the narrative, the device of the deceased grandmother alerts the reader to the significance of the spirit world for interpreting and mapping different networks of narrative value and possibility. That the awful grandmother needs, in Bill Johnson Gonzalez's words, "narrative healing" from her living granddaughter further points to the importance of both an embodied and spiritually-attentive narrative practice. Moreover, rather than using the awful grandmother as a simplistic trope of sacred wisdom and organic Mexican culture, *Caramelo* re-orients the narrator's quest for knowledge and identity across various realms of Mexican, Mexican/American, Chicano/a, Latin/a/o, and US popular culture, histories, myths, and family stories that create a sacred, if not easily legible, tapestry of displaced Mexican/American experience.

It is this narrative remix and the multiple border-crossings and displacements represented in *Caramelo* that prompt scholars to interpret the novel as providing a transnational commentary about Mexican/American identity and experience. For instance, Graf interprets *Caramelo* as a translation of the telenovela form or a "Mexicanized melodrama," while Bill Johnson González focuses on Celaya's unique and literal translations from Spanish to English as crafting a place from which to "mount a critique in two directions" (Graf 1, Johnson González 5). Likewise, Juanita Heredia focuses on the novel's ability to critique the politics of gender on both sides of the US-Mexico border and Celaya's ability to craft her own "third culture" at the border. (See also Calderon 2004). As Melamed and other critics have argued, however, the tendency toward this type of transnational reading also lends itself to neoliberal interpretations that valorize a mobile, culturally diverse and aware subject such as Celaya, and the novel's ability to convey this experience and knowledge to mainstream readers. To the contrary, *Caramelo*'s scope of storytelling and the sedimented layers of cultural, spiritual, political, and familial histories it unearths, far exceed the parameters of nation states and, therefore, highlight more than a mix or critique of two national cultures. Moreover, the networks of icons and stories that *Caramelo* crafts easily surpass the temporal boundaries of Celaya's immediate family, making the story less about a contemporary response to recent migrations as it is about documenting the affective experience of over a hundred years of displacement. Turning to a spiritual realm that exceeds national and temporal boundaries helps to convincingly represent the impact of this kind of physical, spiritual, and emotional displacement. The fact that the narration nonetheless has such a present-ness to it furthers my assertion that the text documents a felt experience in the borderlands that cannot be literally transcribed, but that nonetheless exists and is captured in the novel's spiritually attentive and often pleasurable narrative practice.

## A SPIRITUALLY ACTIVE NARRATIVE MAP

I'd like to look now at a key example of *Caramelo*'s spiritual activism—the narrative map of popular culture that Celaya constructs throughout the novel. As I've alluded, *Caramelo* offers a prodigious narration of family stories, biographies, sayings, histories, and myths, and the cumulative effect is a narrative map of otherwise invisible Mexican/American and Latin/o/a American popular history, culture, and beliefs. One of the most striking aspects of this "map" is its rapid juxtaposition of anecdotes about US, Latina/o, Mexican, Mexican/American, Latin American, and Pan-American iconic or celebrity figures and culture. From the obscure stories of US-born entertainer Yolanda "Tongolele" Montes to the Mexican-but-Americanized icon Rita Hayworth, and from glosses of Mexican melodramatic films, comics, and the Llorona myth to the Spanish ventriloquist Señor Wences, these are just a few of the icons that bear as much narrative importance as the stories of Celaya's own family members. For some critics, this plurality of stories was acutely felt as a lack of coherence. Referring to the novel's audio version, Ann Burns writes, "These tapes require one's full attention, but the tale (with much repetition and snail pace progression, hence little drama) refuse to captivate" (71). But from the perspective of Anzaldúa's spiritual activism, the re-narration of these (largely female) icons from the Global South alongside the intergenerational stories of the Reyes's Pan-American past brings a much-needed sanctity and pleasure to Celaya's act of female storytelling that does not default to an "authentic" or easily legible Mexican/American, Chicano/a or Mexican identity.

In Desiree Martín's study of Chicano/a culture and what she calls "secular sanctity," she notes the close proximity of sacred and celebrity culture. In order for a story, practice, or individual to be deemed sacred, it needs to be in relationship with a public. As Martín explains, "Both saints and celebrities require the adulation of the public for their very existence" (20). Following this line of thinking, we can see how Cisneros's lively and superfluous map of popular icons performs a sort of hagiography of Latin/a/o cultural expression and storytelling that cannot be reduced to a single and authoritative Mexican or Chicano/a ethnic identity, but that is anchored in the diverse, displaced, and re-placed experiences of the diaspora. The social and yet sacred quality of culture, and narrative in particular, is further increased by the intertwining of the deceased grandmother's interjections, as well as by Celaya's references to "la divina providencia," or divine providence (aptly gendered female), as the best storyteller of them all. Together, these devices not only map otherwise-ghosted and complex experiences of the Mexican diaspora, but they begin to construct an alternative network of cultural value that attempts to index the often-overlooked pleasurable and healing aspects of storytelling and, therefore, push back against existing neoliberal frameworks of aesthetic value and interpretive transaction. As Alumbaugh explains: "Any reader has to be willing to traverse linguistic, cultural, and epistemological boundaries in order to fully reckon with the complexity of [*Caramelo*'s] migratory narrative" (72).

Of course, many artists and cultural critics have attempted to articulate these less-tangible aspects of cultural expression as a way to locate its distinctive value (see Hungerford 2010, Benjamin 1968). The distinguishing feature of spiritual activism in *Caramelo*, however, is that its assertion of storytelling as a sacred act does not consequently distance itself from the body or from materiality. In fact, while the myriad popular Mexican/American and Latin/a/o references constellate a veritable hagiography, many of the individual nodes (or stories) on Celaya's narrative map locate the very bodily, material, and political aspects of expressive culture. For instance, *Caramelo*'s stories plot the physical locations across the Americas where artists worked while rising to fame, they tell the tales of artists' economic downturns, and they recuperate the everyday livelihoods of those who worked in and around the arts (275, 192, 229). The novel also shows how desire factors into cultural production by archiving the pop culture destinies of Josephine Baker, whose "destiny" drastically changes upon meeting her lover Billy Baker, and the many artists (including Frida Kahlo) who were romantically involved with the female singer Pánfila Palafox (142, 181). In the world of *Caramelo*, stories and culture permeate and influence our economic, political, and romantic lives, and vice versa. And, in the case of a Mexican diasporic subject such as Celaya, stories and culture can provide the raw material for carving a narrative (and artistic) sense of place in the face of decades of displacement. *Caramelo*'s narrative map attests to the mental and spiritual terrain of diasporic subjects whose sense of home cannot be located firmly in the physical world. As Celaya reflects near the end of the novel: "…these things, that song, that time, that place, are all bound together in a country I am homesick for, that doesn't exist anymore. That never existed. A country I invented. Like all emigrants caught between here and there" (434). As the narrative map in *Caramelo* attests, this place does exist and it is constantly being shaped by Celaya through her creative will, which provides pleasure and meaning to an existence that does not fall neatly along politically charged notions of identity and belonging.

As I've suggested, spiritual activism emerges from Anzaldúa's work on identity, spirituality, cultural expression, and political engagement and places significant emphasis on an embodied, social, and spiritually-informed way of being. A spiritually active perspective and practice does not erect mutually exclusive boundaries around the realms of artistic or cultural production, economics, spirituality, or social interaction. Correspondingly, Cisneros's careful curation of Mexican/American and Latin/a/o popular culture and family stories makes it all but impossible for readers to pin down a "real," easily legible experience of the Mexican diaspora.

## CONCLUSION

References to the "spirit" or what it means to document and communicate with the unseen are typically deemed incomprehensible by the dominant culture, especially when they do not align with moneymaking imperatives. In Joseph Murphy's 2015 study of the widespread growth of botánicas, or Latina/o religious stores, across the US, he notes the opacity and deep misunderstanding with which many non-Latina/o observers see these spaces. These enclaves, however, represent deep layers of different Pan-American spiritualties that take root, usually in the barrios of major US cities, and attest to the presence and experience of their Latina/o and African American patrons. Moreover, the carefully curated collection of devotional items inside the stores—candles, oils, statues, books, potions—and the detail with which the shop owner prescribes these to patrons become the foundation for the stores' success and longevity. Referring to this interpersonal and interspiritual practice, Murphy quotes a study from the 1960s that concludes: "…[the botánica's] program is bringing more hope, security, satisfaction, and happiness to the [barrio] than all the 'poverty programs' vainly attempting to solve urban problems" (Winslow qtd. in Murphy 20). While there is certainly room for multiple restorative programs and, better yet, systemic changes to end the cycle of oppression in Latina/o communities, this quote points to a different value system at play via the local botánicas. In a sense, *Caramelo* is involved in a similar curating process except with overlooked Latin/a/o stories and icons that represent different layers of Mexican diasporic identity—some inherited, some self-chosen—that Cisneros arranges in ways that activate their empowering qualities while still acknowledging their limitations. After all, these stories and icons are all in motion with each other and provide flashes of meaning in one configuration, only to be rearranged shortly thereafter. The ending, however, attests to the ongoing power of its spiritually active narrative with a tongue-in-cheek promise that the narrator will not re-tell her family's stories, suggesting that storytelling will indeed be a continual, defiant, and pleasurable activity. Unlike Melamed's "race radical" texts, *Caramelo* does not provide the key to or a one-to-one representational map for social change. Instead, Cisneros's spiritual activism (like that of the botánica workers) attests to the invisible, but meaningful network that Latina/o narrative and culture already inhabit even as that network is always already incomplete.

## NOTES

1. According to AnaLouise Keating, who is among those in charge of Anzaldúa's estate, "Anzaldúa had carefully packed and stored these materials in every room of her house in Santa Cruz, California" ("Archival" 161).

2. While I use "Mexican/American" to reference the ethnic specificity of the subjects in *Caramelo*, I do not use it to describe the felt experiences of displacement that the novel attempts to map and narrate. The spiritually active narrative, by default, wrestles with the imprecise experiences and identities of the subjects in the novel and the need to record and express them. Correspondingly, I refer to *Caramelo*'s spiritually active narrative map as Latin/o/a, thereby indicating the many influences and histories it draws from. Like Anzaldúa's spiritual concept of nepantla, which she describes as "un lugar no-lugar" [a place that is no place], the narrative works in fleshing out this uncharted, multi-dimensional experience ("Spiritual Activism" 1). Additionally, as is common in the field, I use the term "Latina/o" when speaking about the academic and marketing enterprise of literary and artistic culture produced by artists who descend from Spanish-speaking regions.

3. Other scholars addressing neoliberalism and literary culture include Roderick Ferguson's *The Re-Order of Things: The University and its Pedagogies of Difference* (2012), which studies the way that the university operates as an archival force that incorporates but also regulates difference, and the way that minority cultural forms and practices represent complex relationships between institutionality and textuality in a post-civil rights time period (16). Also, Michael Dowdy's more recent *Broken Souths: Latina/o Poetic Responses to Neoliberalism and Globalization* (2013) stands alone in focusing on Latina/o literary culture and gives equal consideration to the way that minority literary production has responded creatively to the constraints and effects of neoliberalism while still taking into consideration the institutional role of "mechanisms of literary production" (ix).

4. Beginning with post-WWII literary production and concluding with the post-2000 literature of the "neoliberal multicultural" era, Melamed details a range of co-opting forces that pivot around the university, as well as a handful of "race radical" texts that work against the aforementioned disciplinary tactics.

5. In this essay, queerness is not solely a reference to non-heterosexual sex, but also indexes unexamined, uncharted, and visionary social and political relations. Following José Muñoz, queerness can "[exist] for us as an ideality that can be distilled from the past and used to imagine the future" (1). Under this formulation, queerness is also, importantly, performative. As Muñoz explains, "it is not simply a being but a doing for and toward the future" (1). I also draw on Martin Manalansan's notion of "queerness as mess," which poignantly captures the "material and affective conditions of impossible subjects as well as an analytical stance that negates, deflects, if not resists the 'cleaning up' function of the normative" ("The Messy").

## WORKS CITED

Alumbaugh, Heather. "Narrative Coyotes: Migration and Narrative Voice in Sandra Cisneros *Caramelo.*" *MELUS*, vol. 35, no. 1, spring 2010, pp. 53–75.

Anzaldúa, Gloria. *Borderlands/La Frontera: The New Mestiza.* 3rd ed., Aunt Lute, 2007.

---. "Spiritual Activism: Making Altares, Making Connections, 1999." Gloria Evangelina Anzaldúa Papers, Benson Latin American Collection, University of Texas Libraries, the University of Texas at Austin. Box 64, folder 20.

Benjamin, Walter. "The Work of Art in the Age of Mechanical Reproduction." *Illuminations: Essays and Reflections*, edited by Hannah Arendt, translated by Harry Zohn, Harcourt Brace, 1968, pp. 217–251.

Bost, Suzanne. "Messy Archives and Materials that Matter: Making Knowledge with the Gloria Anzaldúa Papers." *PMLA*, vol. 130, no. 3, 2015, pp. 615–630.

Burns, Ann. "Caramelo." *Library Journal*, vol. 128, no. 7, 15 April 2003, p.146.

Calderón, Hector. "Como Mexico No Hay Dos: Sandra Cisneros's Feminist Border Studies." *Narratives of Greater Mexico: Essays on Chicano Literary History, Genre, and Borders*, U of Texas P, 2004, pp. 167–213.

Cisneros, Sandra. *Caramelo*. Alfred A. Knopf Press, 2002.

Dávila, Arlene. *Culture Works: Space, Value, and Mobility Across the Neoliberal Americas*, New York UP, 2012.

Delgadillo, Theresa. *Spiritual Mestizaje: Religion, Gender, Race, and Nation in Contemporary Chicana Narrative.* Duke UP, 2011.

Dowdy, Michael. "Introduction: Contesting the Counter-Revolution." *Broken Souths: Latina/o Poetic Responses to Neoliberalism and Globalization*, U of Arizona P, 2013, pp. 1–28.

Ferguson, Roderick. *The Re-Order of Things: The University and its Pedagogies of Minority Difference.* U of Minnesota P, 2012.

Graf, Amara. "Mexicanized Melodrama: Sandra Cisneros' Literary Translation of the Telenovela in *Caramelo.*" *Label Me Latina/o*, vol. 4, Fall 2014, pp. 1–20.

Harvey, David. "Introduction." *A Brief History of Neoliberalism*, Oxford UP, 2007, pp. 1–4.

Heredia, Juanita. "Voyages South and North: The Politics of Transnational Gender Identity in *Caramelo* and *American Chica*," *Latino Studies*, vol. 5, 2007, pp. 340–357.

Hungerford, Amy. "Introduction: Belief in Meaninglessness." *Postmodern Belief: American Literature and Religion Since 1960*, Princeton UP, 2010, pp. xiii–xxx.

Johnson González, Bill. "The Politics of Translation in Sandra Cisneros's *Caramelo.*" *Differences: A Journal of Feminist Cultural Studies*, vol. 17, no. 3, 2006, pp. 3–19.

Keating, AnaLouise. "'I'm a Citizen of the Universe': Gloria Anzaldúa's Spiritual Activism as Catalyst for Social Change." *Feminist Studies* vol. 35, nos. 1/2, Spring/Summer 2008, pp. 53–69.

---. "Archival Alchemy and Allure: The Gloria Evangelina Anzaldúa Papers as Case Study." *Aztlán: A Journal of Chicano Studies*, vol. 35, no. 2, 2010, pp. 159–171.

Manalansan, Martin, IV. "The Messy Itineraries of Queerness." *Cultural Anthropology*, 21 July 2015. https://culanth.org/fieldsights/705-the-messy-itineraries-of-queerness, Accessed 13 March 2017.

Martín, Desiree. *Borderlands Saints: Secular Sanctity in Chicano/a and Mexican Culture*. Rutgers UP, 2013.

Melamed, Jodi. *Represent and Destroy: Rationalizing Violence in the New Racial Capitalism*. U of Minnesota P, 2011.

Muñoz, José Esteban. *Cruising Utopia: The Then and There of Queer Futurity*. New York UP, 2009.

Murphy, Joseph F. *Botánicas: Sacred Spaces of Healing and Devotion in Urban America*. UP of Mississippi, 2015.

Yúdice, George. *The Expediency of Culture: Uses of Culture in the Global Era*. Duke UP, 2003.

# THE COYOLXAUHQUI IMPERATIVE IN DEVELOPING COMUNIDAD-SITUATED WRITING CURRICULA AT HISPANIC-SERVING INSTITUTIONS

YNDALECIO ISAAC HINOJOSA AND CANDACE ZEPEDA

As first-generation college graduates, and, now, Chicanx faculty situated at Hispanic-Serving Institutions (HSIs), we understand all too well what Gloria Anzaldúa means by "haciendo caras," "making faces" as "political subversive gestures" ("Haciendo" xv). Inscribed by social structures, our caras are "marked with instructions on how to be mujer, macho, working class, Chican[x]," more specifically, othered ("Haciendo" xv). Since we were undergraduates at HSIs, academic subcultures (e.g., teachers, advisors, enrollment services, the registrar, student success) taught us to see and understand our bodies as at-risk, remedial, or underprepared. Like tattoos, these adjectives were inscribed onto our body and marked us as targets for discrimination, especially in English composition classrooms where, at times, professors scrutinized or penalized our brown bodies, and curriculum or pedagogy alienated our lived experience or engagement. To survive, each one of us was compelled to wear máscaras, masks to hide the inferiority carved onto our bodies or the incompetence inscribed directly onto our faces. Masks became our way of distinguishing and negotiating us from them or them from us: this nos/otros dichotomy grounded our understanding of being othered and/or broken in some way and forced us to "negotiate cracks between realities," as Anzaldúa maintains ("Geographies" 79). This process helped us to navigate academic spaces and places and served us well to earn that high school diploma, then that BA, MA, PhD, and, eventually, that coveted tenure-track position in a university department of English. On our journeys, we learned, as Anzaldúa says, to "navigate the switchback roads between assimilation/acquiescence to the dominant culture and isolation/preservation of our ethnic cultural identity" ("Geographies" 79). However, from the systematic silencing and shaming of our bodies throughout this process, somewhere along the way, our brown bodies broke from a perpetual state of psychic unrest.

Nonetheless, "may we," as Anzaldúa contends, "do work that matters" and persist ("Let us be" 22). Although we may be broken, our bodies signify a "complex holism" which AnaLouise Keating says is how Anzaldúa represents Coyolxauhqui: "both the acknowledgment of painful fragmentation and the promise of transformative healing" (Anzaldúa, *Light* xxi). In one another, we acknowledge that our complexity as Chicanx rhetoricians working in the discipline of English at HSIs leads us to embrace a Coyolxauhquian nacayotl (body), un cuerpo that embraces that "necessary process of dismemberment and fragmentation," as Anzaldúa maintains, and "of seeing that self or the situations you're embroiled in differently" ("Let us be" 19–20). It is our individual responsibility, as a Coyolxauhquian nacayotl, to question how our institutions respond to students who have been oppressed by their color, or inscribed with similar labels of inferiority.[1]

Further, as members of a discipline historically rooted in rhetorical acts of white consciousness (Sandoval 126–127), we acknowledge that we work against a history of educational ideologies that (grossly) established the dominance of a Standard English language, which ultimately disempowered and shamed the linguistic heritage and cultural wealth of students not only oppressed, but also marginalized by their color. We contend that this ideological model is subtly preserved in the field of writing studies that, more often than not, continues to perpetuate a Eurocentric narrative that students must master academic discourse to gain entrance into the academy (Althusser, Bartholomae, Castillo, Clifford, Gee). Considering the current scholarship, relatively few mainstream scholars in writing studies present alternative approaches to acknowledging the epistemologies of students who feel compelled to wear máscaras in silence, especially at HSIs where the majority have become minoritized.

By not only embracing our understanding of ourselves but also enacting a Coyolxauhquian nacayotl, we offer insight on the pedagogical value of deconstructing and constructing academic spaces to accommodate students oppressed by their color, with special attention to Latinx students. We present approaches—habits of mind, if you will—for practitioners to decolonize hegemonic spaces and identify ways in which students of different racial and ethnic backgrounds utilize literacy to negotiate, resist, and even transform their local communities. We also recognize HSIs as nepantlas—contested spaces set firmly in-between serving Hispanic (Latinx) students and serving institutions wielding hegemonic discourses. Our focus is specific to how such oppressive discourses may operate in writing classrooms, because to teach writing using hegemonic conventional practices is to teach fundamental lessons about "being" in the world (Yagelski). We adopt Anzaldúa's Coyolxauhqui imperative as a methodology to counter such practices. First, we deconstruct hegemonic conventional practices, and, second, we seek to reconstruct those practices in a way that connects learning with students' lives. When geographical boundaries no longer define borders necessarily, or when Latinx populations are no longer defined solely by their ethnic/racial status, students must come to understand their own subjectivity, to see themselves or their situations differently, and to understand how institutions help to shape and reshape ideologies. It is for this reason that we developed comunidad-situated writing curricula that rely on Anzaldúan theories to emphasize community literacy that encourages equity, sustainability, and social justice.

## HISPANIC-~~SERVING~~ -SHAMING INSTITUTIONS

Hispanic-Serving Institutions (HSIs) are the fastest-growing minority-serving institutions in the nation, increasing from 242 institutions to 409 in a span of ten years (from 2004 to 2014) and enrolling 64% of all Latinx undergraduates in the nation ("Hispanic-Serving Institutions"). With such rapid growth, first-generation, Latinx students who enter these institutional spaces may experience shame more often than not, as we did. Even though Latinx students (often first-generation) make up a large population of HSIs (sometimes close to half of undergraduate enrollment), data illustrates that these students do not graduate at the same national rate as White students. Compared to Whites, who complete college at a rate that varies between 62 and 63%, Emily Tate reports that Latinx graduation rates vary between 38 and 45%. These rates also may not reflect accurately the growing number of Latinx students who leave college before graduation due to a variety of reasons, including, but not limited to: financial costs associated with rising tuition; a lack of mentors; inability to academically acculturate; or the stress of juggling families, jobs, and school simultaneously.[2] We question if these educational sites are truly evaluating how they *serve* the increasing number of Latinx students who populate them. Understanding the role HSIs play in accelerating Latinx graduation rates is happening with some frequency with demographers, educational leadership, and policy analysts, but these conversations are not occurring at the same rate in academic disciplines. Few scholars in the field of writing studies question the institutional priorities, or lack thereof, of HSIs and their ability to respond to a diverse student population.

In 2007, writing studies scholar Michelle Hall Kells argued, "Hispanic Serving Institutions are the most underserved and unrecognized sites for teaching, research, and educational activism" (viii). More than fourteen years later, in her book titled *Reclaiming Composition for Chicano/as and Other Ethnic Minorities: A Critical History and Pedagogy*, Iris Ruiz asserts that

> merely enabling an institution to reflect more diversity in its curricula does not necessarily mean that action will be taken to change curricula. Indeed, oftentimes, the curricula stays the same as it was prior to receiving HSI funds and recognition...the curriculum does not reflect the needs of this population as far as being ethnically empowering or relevant to their cultural backgrounds. (128)

In writing studies (also known as composition studies), Ruiz and Kells are among a few scholars who question the institutional priorities of HSIs. We echo their inquiries and others who argue that the "'Hispanic-serving' designation can be seen to be an acquired identity—that is, one that results from demographic changes that happen ***to*** the institution and not necessarily purposeful action ***by*** the institution" (Bolded emphasis in original, Malcom, Bensimon, and Dávila 2). For instance, the absence of continued faculty and staff development on how to work with first-generation, low-income, Latinx students is obvious when encountering conversations on campuses about these students. More frequently, staff and faculty resort to a deficit-based discourse when discussing Latinx students as "'Incapable of learning,' 'Not college material,' 'Speaking with accents,' 'High risk,' 'High maintenance,' 'Disadvantaged,' 'Remedial,' 'Underprepared,' or 'Culturally deprived'" (Rendón, et al. 4). These phrases and labels continue to preserve the shaming of students marginalized or oppressed by their color or social status and continue to perpetuate their silencing. What this discourse does not acknowledge are the assets (or ventajas) that Latinx students bring into the classroom. These assets are not necessarily those accumulated through formal education but those gained from lived experiences, cultural traditions, and life challenges, all which help students overcome obstacles (Rendón, et al. 4).

In our view, HSIs, like Coyolxauhqui, are broken spaces and must be held responsible for reevaluating their approaches when 'serving' students marginalized by their color, because without an intense examination of how to improve their dialogue, HSIs risk encouraging the shaming of particular populations of students. We encourage comunidad-situated dialogues that welcome a "focus on Latin@ cultural wealth and experiential ways of knowing that students employ to transcend their socioeconomic circumstances and to excel in education" (Rendón, et al. 4). A shift like this in discourse practices would align with Chicana feminist scholarship that brings attention to subjective politics and holistic education. This approach to learning and how one achieves consciousness is a constant theme in Anzaldúa's work, specifically through her stages on the path to conocimiento. In addition, her interpretation of the Coyolxauhqui imperative as a symbolic process for individuals to reconstruct and construct their identities as a method for healing could provide practitioners with a heuristic for re-evaluating how best to serve Latinx students who find themselves displaced at HSIs. Borrowing this approach of reconstructing/

constructing, we offer four approaches that may help practitioners at HSIs to develop and shape what we identify as comunidad-situated writing curricula.

## COMUNIDAD-SITUATED WRITING CURRICULA

For Anzaldúa, the Coyolxauhqui imperative is "the act of calling back those pieces of the self/soul that have been dispersed or lost, the act of mourning the losses that haunt us" (*Light* 1–2). It is through this act that Anzaldúa finds the motivation to "process" these struggles and to "'write out'" such experiences (*Light* 2). Therefore, for Anzaldúa, the Coyolxauhqui imperative is a means "to heal and achieve integration" ("Let us be" 19). To reach the same goal, we adopt her imperative as a pedagogical goal to help students, specifically for those students who "feel disposable, perpetually unsafe, and torn apart like Coyolxauhqui" (14). We each developed writing curricula designed to situate student bodies back into their local communities, which are, more often than not, displaced or alienated by academia. We call our work "comunidad-situated writing curricula" as it emphasizes community literacy. For instance, Hinojosa built a first-year composition accelerated learning program titled "1301 Plus" at Northwest Vista College in San Antonio, Texas. The curriculum under this program included pedagogy that accounted for students' lived experience and that sought to contextualize students' embodied experiences with reading and writing. Students learned how their literacies were inextricably intertwined with their bodies. Students developed a spatial awareness of how writing takes place, and they began to recognize the possibility of rhetorical action as an outgrowth of their lived experiences. Also, working on a Quality Enhancement Plan (QEP), Zepeda comparably redesigned a developmental, non-credit writing course into a credit-bearing and strength-based course at Our Lady of the Lake University in San Antonio, Texas. The curriculum for this program employs students' experiences as a method to stimulate personal motivation in and out of the classroom. Both courses designed by Hinojosa and Zepeda are writing-intensive and include a writing studio or lab component. Our curricula place great emphasis on the home and community in order to assert how these spaces and places contribute to first-generation epistemologies. The curricula were designed with Coyolxauhqui in mind as a "symbol for reconstruction and reframing" students' experiences in academia and our determination to engage students in an "ongoing process of making and unmaking" that experience ("Let us be" 20). As a result, we employed four approaches to help us design comunidad-situated writing curricula, and we encourage practitioners who teach at HSIs to be mindful of these approaches in developing curricula, especially any curriculum that centers on first-generation students of color in a composition classroom. These approaches include building assignments for developing awareness about spatiality, instilling in students as well as practitioners an attentiveness toward the body, revealing how the body and writing intersect, and finally, identifying rhetorical acts as interactive and relational.

## BUILD ASSIGNMENTS FOR DEVELOPING STUDENTS' SPATIAL AWARENESS

First, we recommend building assignments that aid in helping students develop a spatial awareness about their identity through engaging in creative processes, especially in acts of writing. Developing a spatial awareness about identity means "to cultivate an acute awareness of processes at work in your own psyche and to create symbols and patterns of its operations," as Anzaldúa maintains ("Putting" 95). As practitioners, this imperative means to reconsider traditional methods of instruction and transgress all the rigid boundaries of academic spaces, including teacher-student dynamics. We do so by placing a greater emphasis on students' local conditions, specifically their homes and/or communities, in order to acknowledge how these spaces and places contribute to their own epistemologies, or what Luis Moll et al. refer to as "funds of knowledge," a phrase that refers to culturally developed bodies of knowledge with skills essential for individual functioning (133). Knowledge gained from the home and community, we believe, can be theoretically studied to develop a more holistic, "culturally responsive" pedagogy like Geneva Gay and others advocate.

For example, consider for a moment the ecological design of most Latinx homes and communities as intimate spaces that generate a felt symbolic experience.[3] This position closely aligns with the scholarship of Elisabeth Mermann-Jozwiak, who claims that the "structure of [the] borderlands narrative begins and ends in the private space of 'home'" (48). In *Postmodern Vernaculars*, Mermann-Jozwiak cites Gillian Rose and explains, "Humanist geography has constructed home as a place of attachments… the 'hearth, shelter, home or home base are intimate places to human beings everywhere;' home is 'that special place to which one withdraws and from which on [sic] ventures forth'" (48). Mermann-Jozwiak shows how, for Chicana authors like Anzaldúa, "home, the literal geographic site, is clearly the place of emotional attachments" (48).

Editors of *Chicana/Latina Education in Everyday Life* point out that the need to re-engage educational scholarship to include the lived experiences of Latinxs in classrooms is crucial. In doing so, we encourage practitioners to engage the sensibilities that students bring to school from their sources of knowledge. Families and communities, according to the editors, are "central to their children's socialization and to community processes of empowerment" (2). By transforming writing classrooms into familiar community spaces (spaces of comunidad), students are capable of bridging home-based knowledge with academic experiences, thus empowering their authority as writers in an institutional culture.

To illustrate how practitioners can draw on homes and communities as a means for developing a spatial identity, we ask students to write about two distinct art landscape depictions and then encourage a discussion about spatial awareness within the environments depicted. Both images present a different emotional understanding of space and memory, but only one image closely relates to the understanding of home or community for most Latinx students. For these students, who comprise at least 25% or more at HSIs, conversations about each piece of art often result in a feeling or sense of unfamiliarity or symbolic disconnect with the landscape in Georges Seurat's *A Sunday on la Grande Jatte* and a feeling or sense of familiarity or symbolic connection with the landscape in Carmen Lomas Garza's *Barbacoa para Cumpleaños*. Garza's portrayal of images of a family gathering or cookout is very familiar and/or symbolic of home and community felt by most Latinx students (e.g., piñata, fabric, barbeque pit).

These juxtaposed images may help to illustrate that for first-generation Latinx students, bodies matter and how the situated nature of bodies to places matter most in relation to how those places are felt. For most Latinx students, writing classrooms are generally unfamiliar spaces disconnected from their reality, but any discussions about how spaces present and represent felt symbolic experiences will help to show how subjects are "positioned through language" (Clifford 384). This connection further supports Mary Pat Brady's position on space and place as "felt and experienced," and "the processes producing space therefore also shape feelings and experiences" (8). For Brady, "spaces felt" are understood, envisioned, defined, and experienced (7), but a closer understanding of such spaces as Brady describes needs to address the body in the way that other feminist scholars such as Paula M.L. Moya and feminist geographers such as Doreen Massey argue.

## INSTILL ATTENTIVENESS TOWARD THE BODY

We also recommend shedding some light on the significance of having attentiveness toward the body. "Language and rhetoric have a persistent material aspect that demands acknowledgement," according to Jack Selzer, "and material realities often (if not always) contain a rhetorical dimension that deserves attention: for the language is not the only medium or material that speaks" (8). Since Selzer points to language as having a material aspect and that material realities have a rhetorical dimension, materiality merits an examination, then, over how such materiality is imposed rhetorically onto the body, either corporeal or discursive, for rhetoric "acts on the whole person—body as well as mind—and often on the person situated in a community of other persons," according to Carole Blair (46). This perspective grounds our curriculum development in a theory in the flesh, keeping in mind that Moraga and Anzaldúa argued for a theory built upon physical realities. As a material rhetoric, physical realities (or material realities) are particularly important for us to consider as practitioners in writing studies when it comes to writing instruction or writing pedagogy, especially in and with a particular location, or rather HSI context, in mind because "[t]o neglect these material realities... is to ignore the politics of space," as Nedra Reynolds notes (248).

To explain, we refer to Chicana feminists like Anzaldúa who illustrate best how one may possess a broken body. By rendering their bodies into "one of process and connection, of interrelatedness," they offer alternative spatial configurations (Brady 152). They propose a "theoretics of space," which, according to Brady, "implicates the production of space in the everyday, in the social, but that unlike many space theories suggests the relevance of aesthetics, or 'the literary mode of knowing' for understanding the intermeshing of the spatial and the social" (6). The incorporation of aesthetics extends spatial critiques as well as the production of space and of identities. This extension shows a particular attentiveness toward the body. For instance, Brady asserts, "Chicana (and, to some extent, Chicano) literature has been particularly attuned to the complex ways race, gender, sexuality, and class emerge simultaneously, if unevenly, through both the discursive and the spatial" (8). Brady acknowledges how these writers not only engage in the spatialization of bodies but also "explore the spatialization of subjectivities in process, the efforts to fix or to make subjects through their spatialization, as well as how such efforts get deterred" (9). Along these lines, Chicanas offer alternative spatial configurations as they engage in rendering their bodies into "one of process and connection, of interrelatedness" as Brady describes (152). And, a further examination would show how rhetorically their rhetoric falls into processes of negation based on representations of their bodies as broken (i.e., bordered corporeality).

As a bordered corporeality, a broken body signifies a contested site. For example, Katie Conboy, Nadia Medina, and Sarah Stanbury, the editors of *Writing on the Body: Female Embodiment and Feminist Theory*, point out: "the female body [is] a contested site—a battleground for competing ideologies" (7) and "constructed through ideologies, discourses, and practices" (8). This view designates the "body" as a site rendered (made visible) and/or inscribed by materiality and space, and, as such, aligns with Chicana feminists' positions. Thus, Chicana feminists articulate the identification of a discourse that underscores how the body is spatially located and how that specificity influences the evolutionary process of becoming for that body as well as the discursive practices engendered by that body. For instance, Anzaldúa, in the preface to the first edition of *Borderlands/La Frontera*, exemplifies what Conboy et al. suggest and what Chicana feminists articulate:

> I am a border woman. I grew up between two cultures, the Mexican (with a heavy Indian influence) and the Anglo (as a member of a colonized people in our own territory). I have been straddling that *tejas*-Mexican border, and others, all my life. It's not a comfortable territory to live in, this place of contradictions. Hatred, anger and exploitation are the prominent features of this landscape. (19)

Anzaldúa's "border woman" claim in this passage directly indicates how, as a result of being inscribed on her body, spatial and material elements manifest rhetorically from and with her body as a discursive practice. Her phrase is bordered in that it alludes to both a site (border) and a gender (woman). Her statement, "It's not a comfortable territory to live in, this place of contradictions," asserts the explicit positioning(s) of her body as the site contested. The ambiguous "undetermined place" that engenders such bordered corporeality takes place within Anzaldúa's last statement: "Hatred, anger and exploitation are the prominent features of this *landscape*" (emphasis added). If the body is "constructed through ideologies, discourses, and practices," as Conboy et al. suggest, then does Anzaldúa's "landscape" refer to the actual borderland landscape (Tejas-Mexico border) or that of her body (border woman) as the borderland landscape with which she struggles each day? Strategically, this discursive practice positions Anzaldúa's body in a manner that refers to both meanings: place and body.

## REVEAL HOW THE BODY AND WRITING INTERSECT

We recommend revealing how the body and writing intersect, and Anzaldúa's reference about herself as a "border woman" helps us to show that intersection, especially for students from the US-Mexico borderlands area. Anzaldúa's discourse engages and intermingles a corporeality and materiality with and in a given spatiality as they relate to her own broken body, a bordered corporeality. She reveals how a place and a body mutually constitute each other with and in a network of relations; a "border woman" emerges simultaneously both through the spatial and the discursive, which is transcribed from and with her body, a body contested by varied positions at a juncture. Anzaldúa's body represents an extension of the borderlands both figuratively and discursively in her text *Borderlands.*

We can deduce that Chicana subjects, then, occupy bordered corporeality by not only resisting or countering hegemony but also offering an alternate episteme that appeals to their local conditions. For instance, Anna M. Sandoval claims Chicanas "write against a national discourse that does not recognize them" (213) and "often appear to be more critical...of cultural symbols such as La Llorona, La Virgen de Guadalupe, and La Malinche" (214). For example, according to Norma Alarcón, Anzaldúa cuts "across eurohegemonic representations of Woman" by interchanging the names of her resistant subject positions: Snake Woman, La Chingada, Tlazolteotl, Coatlicue, Cihuacoatl, Tonantsi, Guadalupe, La Llorona (119). Alarcón claims that the "polyvalent name-insertions in *Borderlands* is a rewriting of the feminine, a feminist reinscription of gynetics" (119). Similarly, Pérez adds, "Mestizaje, for Anzaldúa, is redefined and remixed into an open consciousness: "'it is a consciousness of the Borderlands' where a 'hybrid progeny' conflates 'racial, ideological, cultural and biological cross-pollination'" (*Decolonial* 25). Therefore, Chicana feminists, like Anzaldúa, instantiate the embodiment of a broken body, like Coyolxauhqui, from discursive practices that are interactive and relational to their subject-position.

## IDENTIFY RHETORICAL ACTS AS INTERACTIVE AND RELATIONAL

Finally, we recommend identifying acts of writing as interactive in that they respond to a complex matrix of activity systems. And, as a result, we connect acts of writing with that "ongoing process of making and unmaking" in Anzaldúa's Coyolxauhqui imperative ("Let us be" 20). The constructing and reconstructing processes of writing involve "gestures of the body" in that "[w]riting is not about being in your head; it's about being in your body," as Anzaldúa says (*Light* 5). Thus, a body engaged in acts of writing constitutes an organic system that occupies space, and with and in that space, the body and the acts of writing are interdependent with each other. Each (the body and the acts of writing) can be seen as two interdependent organisms that operate within an organic environment, where "meaning is triadic" in that "all...are mutually constitutive, mutually dependent," as Kristie S. Fleckenstein notes (166). We recognize this process in how Anzaldúa identifies acts of writing as organic events: "It's not on paper that you create but in your innards, in the gut and out of living tissue—*organic writing* I call it" (emphasis in original, "Speaking in Tongues" 172). Accordingly, Benigno Trigo posits, "'Organic writing' works similarly to alchemy and *condenses* body and language into something different that surprises even the subject who performs it" (emphasis in original 98). The conversion or transformation that takes place between and in-between a body and acts of writing supports our view that writing may be considered as an organism as well within ecology, especially within ecologies of discourse.

As such, we acknowledge acts of writing as interactive rhetorical actions, "rhetoric-as-essentially-related-to situation," as Lloyd F. Bitzer notes (3). Interactive rhetorical actions also underscore where "a particular discourse comes into existence because of some specific condition or situation which invites utterance" (Bitzer 4). Such discourse is characterized by David Foster as exemplifying "the interactive or 'relational' character of discourse," discursive formations not only contextualized within the body and its connection with a specific place but also from symbolic actions inextricably linked with the ecological setting in which such acts manifest (456). Anzaldúa expresses how discourses result from not only her body positioned but also its relation to various ecologies:

> I think we're born with certain predispositions towards ways of being, but the environment also has a lot to do with it—our surroundings, our growing up, and the way ideologies control how we act and think....In this particular community, in this particular race, in this particular time, these are the experiences I'm writing about. (*Interviews* 222)

Anzaldúa contextualizes her rhetorical actions with that which affects her ways of being the most: her body *to* place. Her rhetorical action draws on predispositions toward ways of being as a means to first understand literacy and then make meaning of its material effect on her body, su cuerpo, which is ecologically located amid the discourses *on* and *of* the body within sociocultural contexts. She enacts symbolic actions that respond rhetorically to such discourses not only relational to her position but also in a manner that define and embody her "*distinctive place-identity*, meaningful aspects of identity linked to places felt" (Emphasis in original, Hinojosa 103).

For example, the poem titled "These Hands Which Have Never Picked Cotton" by Chicana poet Amalia Ortiz demonstrates interactive rhetorical actions by illustrating an interdependency that exists between a situated lived experience and a materialized corporeal reality. We refer to this poem to show students how Ortiz articulates a metaphoric body into existence and then inscribes an actualized body already in existence, her own as the speaker writing, by engaging in interactive rhetorical actions. To clarify, "hands" evokes a strong presence of a body's lived experience for Ortiz, and she uses this image as a controlling metaphor to juxtapose first-, second-, and third-generation Latinx experiences:

> these fruitless hands, which have never plucked grapes from the vine
> are strangers to orange groves and grapefruit rows
> these fragile knuckles have never scraped over washboards
> or scrubbed floors for money
> but have been caressed by abuela who did so in my place

Discursively, Ortiz situates the speaker, who identifies as third-generation, in relation to the first and second generation, and she engenders the speaker's identity through the interactions, or lack of interactions, in the speaker's hands: "these hands, which have never picked cotton / become more american at rest." The poem as a discursive formation rhetorically re-presents a situated lived experience for the present. This experience is instantiated into flesh and bone (corporeality) through the corporal forms Ortiz cites:

> this body
> the bones, muscle, youth not yet sacrificed to feed children
> this body understands struggle builds character
> but is still searching for what these hands will build

This situated lived experience not only is instantiated within and from such corporeal forms but also its articulation is distributed across time and space and into the present through a spatialized physicality in what hands can do: "these grateful hands write words of hope / of remembering and being remembered." In this case, the act of writing, of writing to remember and be remembered, is the spatialized physicality Ortiz needs to self-actualize her presence in the poem as a writer through the speaker's action and as a means to stipulate that "this body may not know, but must never forget" within the poem. For Ortiz, this rhetorical act is interactive in that it leaves "a determining mark on the surface" as Homi Bhabha proclaims (9).[4] The mark is discursive evidence that such practices can engender a felt corporeal experience occupying space and co-producing that space. Ortiz and the speaker are mutually constitutive because Ortiz engages spatiality in the poem by intermingling the situated nature of her corporeality with the materiality of her poem. These rhetorical choices made in crafting the poem make Ortiz's symbolic actions within the poem interactive and relational.

## CONCLUSION

Nepantlas embody our Coyolxauhquian nacayotl, and, from our body, we set forth to present the approaches we enact as practitioners working at HSIs. We hope these approaches guide others as they have guided us in developing comunidad-situated writing curricula. Anzaldúa says we are led to "awakening, insights, understandings, realizations, courage, and the motivation to engage in concrete ways with the potential to bring us into compassionate interactions" ("Let us be" 19). And, although we believe HSIs metaphorically represent nepantlas for us based on our experiences and based on our position as agents within that liminal space, we find ourselves torn between ways of serving Latinx students and fearing our acclimation into wielding hegemonic discourses. Thus, we strive to transgress the borders that may sustain us in our commitment to serve as agents of change. Anzaldúa explains,

> Nepantleras are the supreme border crossers. They act as intermediaries between cultures and their various versions of reality.... They serve as agents of awakening, inspire and challenge others to deeper awareness, greater conocimiento, serve as reminders of each other's search for wholeness of being. (Hernández-Avila and Perez 20)

It is for the aforementioned reasons that we are drawn to Anzaldúa's Coyolxauhqui imperative in our work with Latinx students and HSIs. As agents of change, we move to deconstruct and reconstruct not only our own brown identities within such institutions but also our pedagogical practices situated at these institutions of higher education. We do so as a way to always expose how those practices may connect best with students' lived experiences to foster meaningful learning outcomes. Our four approaches contribute to academic conversations that seek to identify ways in which students of different racial and ethnic backgrounds utilize literacy with and in a local context as a means to negotiate, resist, and even transform local communities. We encourage practitioners to consider these comunidad-situated dialogues: to build assignments that develop a sense of spatial awareness, to instill an attentiveness toward the body, to reveal how the body and writing intersect, and to identify rhetorical acts as interactive and relational. We utilized these dialogues as our approaches for developing a comunidad-situated writing curricula at HSIs.

## NOTES

1. *People* or *persons of color* is a phrase used primarily in the United States to describe any non-white individual or to encompass all non-white peoples. The phrase also highlights the systematic racism experienced by people of color. We use the phrase "people oppressed by their color" not just to break the divide between white and non-white, but also to underscore the perpetual degradation of a people based entirely on color.

2. In 2011, Complete College America published a report titled *Time is the Enemy*. The finding of this report reveals that poor students and students of color struggle the most to graduate and that the new American majority (75%) on college campus are students who juggle a combination of families, jobs, and school while commuting to class.

3. We use intimacy in relation to Anzaldúa's perception of the discursive formation of language as a living and intimate act (*Borderlands* 19–20). For Anzaldúa, writing allows her to "become more intimate with [herself]" (*Gloria Anzaldúa Reader* 30).

4. Homi Bhabha refers to writing as a political form where writing may be the "possibility of making a determining mark on the surface," as in the "widest sense:" printed, social, visual, etc. (9).

## WORKS CITED

Althusser, Louis. "Ideology and Ideological State Apparatuses: (Notes Toward an Investigation)." 1971. *Lenin and Philosophy and Other Essays*. Translated by Ben Brewster, Monthly Review Press, 2001, pp. 127–86.

Anzaldúa, Gloria. *Borderlands/La Frontera: The New Mestiza*. 1987. 2nd ed., Aunt Lute, 1999.

---. "Geographies of Selves – Reimagining Identity: No/Otraas (Us/Other), las Nepantleras, and the New Tribalism." *Light in the Dark*, pp. 65–94.

---. *The Gloria Anzaldúa Reader*. Edited by AnaLouise Keating, Duke UP, 2009.

---. "Haciendo Caras, Una Entrada." *Making Face, Making Soul/Haciendo Caras: Creative and Critical Perspectives by Feminists of Color*, edited by Gloria Anzaldúa, Aunt Lute, 1990, pp. xv–xxviii.

---. *Interviews/Entrevistas*. Edited by AnaLouise Keating, Routledge, 2000.

---. "Let us be the healing of the wound: The Coyolxauhqui imperative—La sombra y el sueño." *Light in the Dark*, pp. 9–22.

---. *Light in the Dark/ Luz en lo Oscuro: Rewriting Identity, Spirituality, Reality*, edited by AnaLouise Keating, Duke UP, 2015.

---. "Putting Coyolxauhqui Together: A Creative Process." *Light in the Dark*, pp. 95–116.

---. "Speaking in Tongues: A Letter to Third World Women Writers." *This Bridge Called My Back: Writings by Radical Women of Color*, edited by Cherríe Moraga and Gloria Anzaldúa. 2nd ed., Kitchen Table: Women of Color Press, 1983, pp. 165–74.

Bartholomae, David. "Inventing the University." *Cross-Talk in Comp Theory*. 2nd ed., edited by Victor Villanueva, National Council of Teachers of English, 2003 pp. 623–53.

Bernal, Dolores Delgado, et al., editors. *Chicana/Latina Education in Everyday Life: Feminista Perspectives on Pedagogy and Epistemology*, State U of New York P, 2006, pp. 113–32.

Bhabha, Homi K. *The Location of Culture*. 1994. Routledge, 2006.

Bitzer, Lloyd F. "The Rhetorical Situation." *Philosophy & Rhetoric*, vol. 25, no. 1, 1992, pp. 1–14.

Blair, Carole. "Contemporary U.S. Memorial Sites as Exemplars of Rhetoric's Materiality." *Rhetorical Bodies*, edited by Jack Selzer and Sharon Crowley, U of Wisconsin P, 1999. 16–57.

Brady, Mary Pat. *Extinct Lands, Temporal Geographies: Chicana Literature and the Urgency of Space*, Duke UP, 2002.

Castillo, Ana. *Massacre of the Dreamers: Essays on Xicanisma*, Plume Press, 1994.

Clifford, John. "The Subject is Discourse." *Relations, Locations, Positions: Composition Theory for Writing Teachers*, edited by Peter Vandenberg et al., National Council of Teachers of English, 2006, pp. 381–99.

Fleckenstein, Kristie S. *Embodied Literacies: Imageword and a Poetics of Teaching*. Southern Illinois UP, 2003.

Foster, David. "What Are We Talking About When We Talk About Composition." *The Norton Book of Composition Studies*, edited by Susan Miller. Norton, 2009, pp. 451–60.

Gay, Geneva. *Culturally Responsive Teaching: Theory, Research, and Practice*. Teachers College, 2010.

Gee, James Paul. *Situated Language: A Critique of Traditional Schooling*. Routledge, 2004.

Hernández-Avila, Inés, and Domino Perez. "Speaking Across the Divide." *SAIL: Studies in American Indian Literatures*, vol. 15, nos. 3–4, Fall 2003–Winter 2004, pp. 7–22.

Hinojosa, Yndalecio Isaac. "Localizing the Body for Practitioners in Writing Studies." *El Mundo Zurdo 5: Selected Works from the 2015 Meeting of the Society for the Study of Gloria Anzaldúa*, edited by Domino Renee Perez et al., Aunt Lute Books, 2016, pp. 101–10.

"Hispanic-Serving Institutions (HSIs): 2015–2016." *Excelencia in Education*, Mar. 2017, www.edexcelencia.org/media/184.

Kells, Michelle Hall. Foreword. *Teaching Writing with Latino/a Students: Lessons Learned at Hispanic-Serving Institutions*, edited by Cristiana Kirklighter et al., State U of New York P, 2007, pp. vii–ix.

Massey, Doreen. *Space, Place, and Gender*. U of Minnesota P, 1994.

Merman-Jozwiak, Elizabeth. *Postmodern Vernaculars: Chicana Literature and Postmodern Rhetoric*. Peter Lang, 2005.

Malcom, Lindsey E., et al. "(Re)Constructing Hispanic-Serving Institutions: Moving Beyond Numbers Toward Student Success." *Education Policy and Practice Perspectives*, vol. 6, Winter 2010, pp. 1–8.

Moll, Luis C., et al. "Funds of Knowledge for Teaching: Using a Qualitative Approach to Connect Homes and Classrooms." *Theory into Practice*, vol. 31, no. 2, Spring 1992, pp. 132–42.

Moya, Paula M.L. *Learning from Experience: Minority Identities, Multicultural Struggles*. U of California P, 2002.

Ortiz, Amalia. *Rant. Chant. Chisme*. Wings Press, 2015.

Rendón, Laura I., et al. *Ventajas/Assets y Conocimientos/Knowledge: Leveraging Latin@ Strengths to Foster Student Success*. Center for Research and Policy in Education, The University of Texas at San Antonio, 2014.

Reynolds, Nedra. "Composition's Imagined Geographies: The Politics of Space in the Frontier, City, and Cyberspace." *Relations, Locations, Positions: Composition Theory for Writing Teachers*, edited by Peter Vandenberg et al., 2006, pp. 226–57.

Ruiz, Iris D. *Reclaiming Composition for Chicano/as and Other Ethnic Minorities: A Critical History and Pedagogy*. Palgrave Macmillan, 2016.

Sandoval, Chela. *Methodology of the Oppressed*. U of Minnesota P, 2000.

Selzer, Jack. "Habeas Corpus: An Introduction." *Rhetorical Bodies*, edited by Jack Selzer and Sharon Crowley. Madison: U of Wisconsin P, 1999, pp. 3–15.

Tate, Emily. "Graduation Rates and Race." *Inside Higher Ed*. 26 Apr. 2017, www.insidehighered.com/news/2017/04/26/college-completion-rates-vary-race-and-ethnicity-report-finds

Trigo, Benigno. *Remembering Maternal Bodies: Melancholy in Latina and Latin American Women's Writing*. Palgrave Macmillan, 2006.

Yagelski, Robert P. *Writing as a Way of Being: Writing Instruction, Nonduality, and the Crisis of Sustainability*. Hampton, 2011.

# NEPANTLA – PRODUCTIONS OF PATHOLOGIES AND HEALING.

## UNDER CONSTRUCTION.

NORMA ALARCÓN, MARISA BELAUSTEGUIGOITIA, AND ROMANA RADLWIMMER

The following pages represent an account of the mesa redonda "Nepantla – Productions of Pathologies and Healing" between Norma Alarcón, Marisa Belausteguigoitia, and Romana Radlwimmer at the International Conference El Mundo Zurdo 2016.[1] The moderator of the mesa redonda was Sara A. Ramírez, and active discussants present in the audience were, among others, María Lugones, Laura Pérez, Sonia Saldívar-Hull, and Josie Méndez-Negrete, Elvia Niebla, and Irene Lara. In our conversation, we ponder the production of cultural, physical, physiological, psychological, emotional, spiritual pathologies as experienced on all levels, for instance, in educational, medical, or political structuring. We approach the pathological states by questioning and affirming the ongoing presence of Eurocentric patriarchy and its contemporary strategies of seduction and the absence of cultural memory of resistance. We reflect on Norma Alarcón's philosophical elaborations on *desire* inside academia and ask in which ways Anzaldúa's *nepantla* can lead us into a state of healing. The healing we envision through the round table is a shared thinking and feeling process along conceptual categories and in a creative space of expression.

**Marisa Belausteguigoitia:** Yesterday, Romana and myself, we thought how exciting it was to have Norma with us. We were thinking of a format for the round table and thought: How can you contain Norma? *(Laughter in the audience)*

**Romana Radlwimmer:** How to contain Norma in a format. *(Laughter in the audience)*

**MB:** A "for-Norma-t" in a way that we could enjoy her and develop a conversation, so we could listen to her and hear each other. We came up with this idea: instead of having a PowerPoint, we are going to have points of power. Ten points of power.

**RR:** Well… it got out of hand… *(Laughter in the audience)*

**Norma Alarcón:** Can we have seven? I prefer seven. *(Laughter in the audience)*

**MB:** We are going to try to generate a conversation—with Sara Ramírez and with you, the public, included—around different issues: texts, definitions, ideas, fashions, and especially with a selection of Anzaldúa's drawings from the Benson Library. Nepantla, la mano zurda, el cuerpo, theory in the flesh—all these concepts that were drawn by Anzaldúa. We know that these drawings came in images in Spanish. We also want to honor that sort of Spanish she spoke, the Spanish of the Southwest, the Spanish of Texas. We will show you some images, and we can react to them.

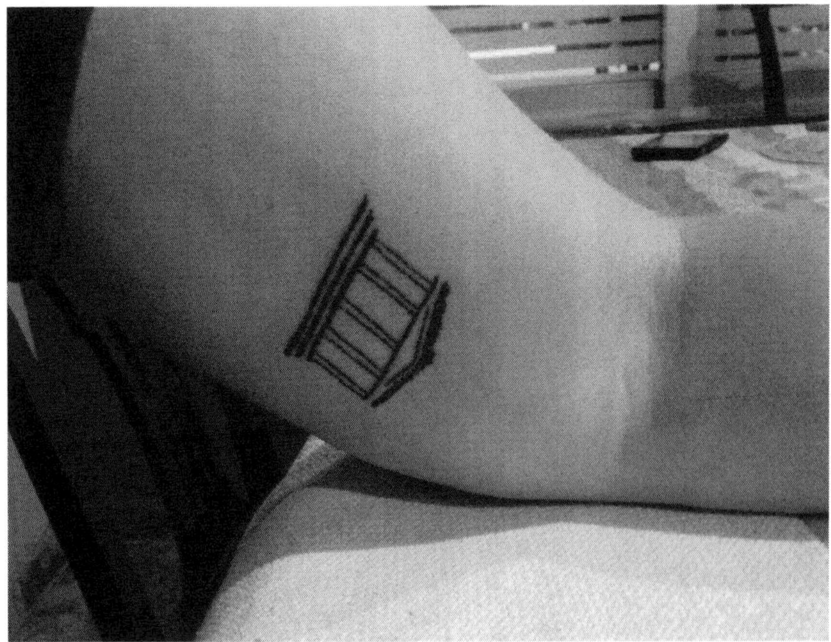

**Figure 1. Photograph of Gelen Alcántara's arm with a tattoo conceptualized as "academia al revés." Photograph courtesy of Marisa Belausteguigoitia.**

So our first point of power shows the upper part of the arm. It shows flesh. It is the arm of one of my students *(shows PowerPoint image with a tattoo)* (See Figure 1). The image represents academia placed upside down, or queer. It is queer, leaning, inclined, atravesada. La academia que se atraviesa, la academia de los atravesados. It is Gelen's arm, one of my former graduate students. Students are, in Mexico and the US, atravesando their sexuality, along conceptual categories, the erotic on the political and the political on the erotic. They are investing in new encounters of desire, but also want to make things appear beyond academic borders: in the political realm, in the aesthetic realm, in the pedagogical, and in the body, the corporeal one. Do you think that students may find in academia, in texts like *Borderlands*, a sort of suspended classroom? A state of interruption of the culturally dominating narratives? A device to think "outside" or at the borders of academia? When do you think that the classroom, as Nepantla, provides an interruption? An interruption of being "Western," being "women," being "students"? Suspend to act upon, to be able to interrupt. The classroom we are working on is a sort of Nepantla–estado suspendido, in Anzaldúa's words—a wider space in their minds. Do students analyzing Anzaldúa in the classroom interact—in Norma's words—with "the construction of political structures of power"? The theory of the practice; the theorizing from the flesh. Now we want reactions on the tattoo of a student, a tattoo turning academia on its head. Puesta de cabeza, o si no: atravesada. Los atravesados en *Borderlands* son los queer, los migrantes. Norma, what do you have to say about academia puesta de cabeza? Is that possible?

**NA:** *(Laughs, then reflective)* Well, it has to be done all over again because it already got started. Eso de ponerla de cabeza, it already got started, when people of color and women started walking, when women of color started walking into the academy. So that already got started. If young people today don't know that, it is because they don't know enough recent history. They don't know the history of the last fifty years. If young people do not know the history of the last fifty or sixty years, then not only are they apparently ignorant, also we have the kind of election we are having right now—*I* think. So, if a student is saying "I am going to put it on its head," I have to say: "It already got started. Catch up." How do you catch up? In doing it again because it's never over. I think it has to be done over and over again for a long time because patriarchy is very solid, very strong. Ponerla de cabeza is a movement, and it is a movement that already started. And if twenty-year-olds feel that they have to do it, yes, they do, but they have to take it up where it already started. And if they don't know about it, they are in trouble, with their lives, let alone the academy: with their lives, their bodies. That doesn't make me feel that the political world is going to turn around or change. We can't do it—those of us who are older. I can't do it. We tried, and we have had our chance. We keep doing it. But if the fifteen- to twenty-year-olds aren't catching up, then we can't turn it upside down again.

**MB:** It will be eventually turned around.

**NA:** I feel that the strength of patriarchy is incommensurable and very devastating to think about, so I don't want to think about it. *(Laughs)*

**MB:** You feel it. You feel it actually in your body. That's part of the pathologies we want to talk about, ¿no?

**Laura Pérez:** When speaking about patriarchy, it seems that there is a new seduction, right? A modernization of patriarchy's techniques, new seductions directed towards women, young women. I have these attacks of perplexity and disbelief when I see the difficulty of penetrating patriarchal thought that views itself as progressive. I think about Bernice [Johnson] Reagon's "coalition is not home," and it helps me to get back up.[2] What are your thoughts about the ways in which patriarchy is seducing?

**NA:** Well, you are already putting your finger on it by calling attention to the cultural consumption and marketing. This is the way it stays in place. This is outside the academy, but it is within a capitalist structure. It is the cultural consumption, rather than just the capitalist structure. They are ahead in the game, incredibly, because they are coming from how to constantly sell something. And they are not going to sell it to me. I mean, they are not going to sell me potato chips or any junk food any more. But it's part of the cultural consumption. It is clothing or food and all of that. It stays in place due to that capitalist structure of consumption and marketing.

**Elvia Niebla:** Isn't it a sign of optimism that we have never had a woman president and now we might have one?

**NA:** Not for me, but I'd rather not talk about that because I don't want to go into American politics.

**RR:** We have been circling around two intriguing fields. The one is desire; the other one is the cultural memory of resistance. These two fields are also linked. Where we are missing the memory of resistance; we have a desire for it. This is relevant to my personal approach to academia. It is closely linked to my academic history. When I first enrolled in European university with the start of the new millennium, a lot changed. The so-called "Bologna process"[3] has altered European university structures and is functioning all over Europe nowadays. The way I tend to construct it today is that in my time as a university student the system was much more open to the study process than it is now. You lived with the sensation that you were able to take the time you needed. You could venture into research at an early stage, into arts, into the interstices between the academy and community, into community. You could follow their connections and create your own artistic and intellectual interstices. There was a certain freedom of time and space. My parents' generation went to universities in the 1960s, the 1970s, y pues metieron caña;[4] they fought for it. Mi generación lo disfrutaba. Yo lo disfrutaba. Until today, academia has ideally been a place of creation and knowledge exchange, an infinite space. This is what I was looking for and what I meant to find, partly. I found thought; I found friendship, so many interesting things. I found—and here we are again with a notion so central to your work, Norma—desire. Desire, as a cultural concept. My desire of finding this infinity. ¿Pero qué tipo de libertad nos puede dar the academy? ¿Qué tipo de libertad nos está negando? Nowadays, in my teaching in Europe, I see the effects of Bologna which established all over a "universal," entre comillas, European system of bachelors and masters, where students have to be very quick, technically quick. It seems that they have to produce and produce, that they are lacking the time to navigate between university and community, lacking the time to go abroad without counting credits and knowing exactly when to return to the foreseen, lacking the time to experience arts, go to the theatres. They prefer to watch their movies at home, and I tell them: What about the experience of going to a critical movie theatre, having discussions there? Or what you told me, María *(asking María Lugones)*, that you were invited to Germany—which I took very personally—and your audience did not discuss anything with you. They invite María Lugones to Germany, and there is no discussion! What does this tell me about my generation, or about this younger in-between generation that you were talking about, Norma? What does this all tell me about the cultural economies produced around consuming? So, the academy is a very ambiguous space for me. Yes, patriarchy is in place, and I agree on the difficulty of recognizing it. It is so well disfrazado… I don't want to use the term "disfrazado." It looks so pretty and colourful, but it's really patriarchy, right?

**MB:** Norma and Romana, you are pointing to the absence of history: the dehistorcizing, dematerializing, and colonizing of history.

**NA:** I am not speaking of history as if I were a historian. I sort of always get in trouble with historians. I say, you are out of my field of discourse. If you are an academic historian, don't even try, okay? *(Laughs and laughter in the audience)*

**MB:** Norma, isn't your elaboration of *desire* a way to interrupt this marketing, and cultural consumption and composition? You are one of the few scholars who elaborate an epistemology of desire. I don't know if I can make this equation: isn't the theory of practice related? The things you *do* with Lacan, Kristeva, and Derrida, you use them to establish some kind of mobile subject-in-process and then you say, "good-bye." You stay with what you exactly need because you know them very well. In the logic of desire there is also a current of Anzaldúa present. You sit Anzaldúa next to Derrida, Kristeva, and Lacan. At the same time, your work is not appropriating that grammar, what you do is not European, es muy… *(Searching for the right expression)*

**NA:** Chueco. *(Laughter in the audience)*

**MB:** Chueco, yes. Well, Lacan is muy europeo.

**NA:** Oh yes.

**MB:** And you—¡Lo pones de cabeza!

**NA:** You want an example of the patriarchy in psychoanalysis: Lacan!

**RR:** Abuelito Lacan.

**MB:** But you had to go through him to talk about desire, y luego desecharlo. I love the way you use patriarchy. You use and dispose it. Los usas y los descartas. We want to pick on your epistemologies and ontologies to unpack lo que dice Laura, que es la constante reinvención de patriarchy, el capitalismo, la estructura de la academia.

**NA:** Well, I was in conversation with Romana a couple of days ago, when I was going through this transformation. *(Points to her orange-purple hair. Laughter in the audience)*

**Audience members:** Looks lovely! Yeah!

**RR:** We went through this transformation together *(points to her pink hair)*, as you might notice. *(More laughter in the audience)*

**NA:** I don't know which hour of the day it was, but I do remember something that she provoked in me, what was true of me, and I said to her: When I was a girl, I wanted to be a reader and a writer. When I was in college, I wanted to be an intellectual, and the only way to be an intellectual in college was through the disciplinary method, getting degrees. I couldn't say, at this point, that my professors were academic intellectuals. Not intellectuals. Some of the philosophers I pick on are intellectuals and never had been academics. I pick them not because of that. It was kind of a being drawn to them. In retrospect, I discovered they were not academics. They never had an academic job. I discovered at an older age that the philosophers I was drawn to did not teach in the academy or did not teach at all. Other than Derrida there was—

**Audience members:** *(Giving philosophers' names)*

**NA:** *(affirming the audience and then offering new names)* Irigaray, Simone de Beauvoir, Hanna Arendt, Cixous, yes, Sartre. Deleuze and Guattari, who were not teaching in any academy. They were invited—that's another story. But it's not being a professor in the academy. I didn't realize that that was my problem *(laughs, and laughter in the audience)*. Academic departments were disciplined. They were disciplinary academics—men and women. From that point of view, women are embedded in the patriarchal structure.

They can call it "gender" or whatever they want to call it, but they are in the patriarchal structure. Here is one way of seeing "gender" as part of the patriarchal structure. When I was in Berkeley in the late '80s, the women grabbed at "gender" really quick because it made them acceptable in the academy. The guys were not going to fight them by using the term "gender." That was okay with the guys—the male professors. Other than that, gender was not relevant. Keep gender out *(laughs)*! That was at least at the time I was there. Back to the story: my problem was that I did not understand that, quote unquote, I liked the intellectual life. The life of thought. What Hanna Arendt called in one of her titles, "The Life of the Mind." I think that is what Gloria, in her own register, liked. And she had no choice but to like it—from my point of view. My point of view on Gloria would be—in me, this might be a point except that she went ahead and did something with it; that she was all her life under the affliction of post-traumatic stress disorder. Post-traumatic stress disorder is a terrific emotional chaos for the person that suffers that. Might get schizophrenic, but might play with it *(laughs)*. I am saying that to Josie Méndez-Negrete, who is pretty well-versed in it. Her research, not herself. *(Laughter in the audience)*

**RR:** In the next point of power, we quote one of your works which reflects on desire and on the mind, which reflects on, as you call it, cognitive desire: "Chicana critics...work in an interstitial zone which is constantly on the move given its structural displacement within the academy."[5] Would you like to comment on that, Norma?

**NA:** I think we have been, since we started here, talking about cognitive desire, maybe even we started our conversation a few days ago. It's constantly on the move because of its constant displacements, so you also have to keep moving. Barbara Smith said in *Bridge* about dealing with white women, having to always say, "Not yet!" and throwing the stone even further. So, we become a politics of "not yet." You haven't got it—*yet*.

**RR:** Okay, I am quoting Norma Alarcón here: "[C]larify what the shift consists of and for whom."[6] What kind of interstitial zone, what kind of Nepantla are we talking about? What shifts are we talking about and between which actors?

**NA:** The interstitial zone—personally, I think—has to be specified by each one of us, by each one of you. Of myself, I can try to specify my interstitial zone. That interstitial zone that we are working, given the displacements, is the one that we are already on track. In other words, our own self-education, as well as our formal education, our own historical moment in time.

**MB:** Could you specify your own interstitial zone?

**NA:** My own interstitial zone?—I had to get out of Berkeley *(laughs and laughter in the audience)* to get my next interstitial zone.

**RR:** And what do pathologies have to do with the interstitial zone?

**NA:** It has to do with embracing the pathologies whatever they are, even if you still don't know what they are. Embrace pathologies. Give up medication. *(Gesturing toward Josie Méndez-Negrete)* If your son, for instance, doesn't want medication, I feel and understand deeply why. With medication, he doesn't feel himself.[7] With medications, at some point you don't know who you really are. One cannot understand and hence embrace pathologies without getting rid of medication.

**RR:** Norma, Marisa, do you—and everybody else in this room—do you think of pathologies as being multilayered, coming in many forms? Medical issues, medications sold as healing; academic questions; institutions. Are these the pathologies? And in which sense are we talking about healing?

**MB:** In other words, what makes us sick?

**RR:** The next point of power shows the Anzaldúan drawing of a hand. La mano zurda connects with the production of pathologies and healing. Would you like to talk about that, Marisa?

**MB:** Pathologies are the underlying theme of this conversation. Gloria Anzaldúa's trabajos, all of them, relate to healing. Norma is a critic intellectual who gives us deep reading, and reading Anzaldúa through Norma is another world. On the point of power, you see the left hand, la mano zurda. Let's not forget what makes us sick, and not forget the position of academia turned upside down. This is what Anzaldúa wrote about the left hand:

> To activate the conocimiento and communication we need the hand. The hand is an agent of action. It is not enough to speak and write and talk and communicate. It is not enough to see and recognize and know. We need to act upon what we know, to do something about it. The left hand has always been sinister and strange, associated with the female gender and creativity. But in unison with the right, the left hand can do great things.[8]

If you look at the point of power, at Anzaldúa's drawing, what do you see in the hand?

**Audience members:** La lengua.

**MB:** La lengua is hanging, like fotografías de la gente cansada. The right to rest is present here. The shape of the tip of the tongue is accentuated, también es muy común decir: lo tengo en la punta de la lengua. At the tip of the tongue. The urgency to spill/spell things out. Los ojos representan an understanding. Pero la lengua es el órgano privilegiado; it is a symbol for breaking silence. And it is a split tongue.

**NA:** I would like to remind us that the privileged sense in European philosophy is linked to the eyes. The visual is the privileged sense of European life.

**An audience member:** Is that the third eye?

**NA:** No, not the third eye.

**RR:** It is the eye coming from above, seeing everything, but not being seen. What comes to mind here is one of the institutional pathologies. It has to do with the first point of power with the academia turned upside down, and Norma and I have had conversations about this. I am referring to the constant construction of distance and superiority. That connects with the eyes you mentioned, Norma: the produced necessity to be up there, to be in control, to go against something, somebody, to watch from a distanced point of view. So, in my perspective, a certain kind of distance is pathological.

**MB:** The left hand is important, what is coming from the left.

**RR:** Yes, that's right, and that is the healing: the left hand as an option for healing. Healing comes through; it means critical intimacy. As Anzaldúa says, not to be detached. Against pathologies, the left hand engages in a process of healing the prevailing visions of distance.

**MB:** La mano zurdo inclina, inclines academia. One of the healing operations could be theorizing from the flesh, activating knowledge, constructing the political structures of experience. In Nepantla classrooms, we are very interested in inclining academia, activating it. Classrooms are disposed with all these texts and all these ways of distancing. But there is also an expected distancing from the academic and from disciplinary thought, in a way of tending to understand things—not yet spelled out—that are at the tip of our tongues. That tip in so many tongues shows—as Norma already pointed brilliantly out— that it already got started. Eso de poner la academia y el mundo de cabeza started when people of color and women of color walked into the academy. It already got started. Norma, you were teaching for so many years.

**NA:** My whole life.

**MB:** The classroom has been a space for you, an interval. Did you feel the magic of your classroom? But *magic* sounds like a soft word: the *power* of your classroom. As students, we were seduced by your power. You did an incredible job in constructing and deconstructing minds, bodies, and desire. Anzaldúa talks about public arts, inner works, compartir. La mano zurda is also the hand that can go into classrooms. Norma, what was your experience?

**NA:** Well, one thing I have to say, especially to younger people, is that I came into a field that was under construction and invention. Two fields really: "ethnic studies" and "women's studies" in general. They were under construction. Even though my formal course work was in the Spanish department at

Indiana University. That was my formal "education." But I was working and playing with two fields that were under construction. That gave me a freedom that others do not have, or cannot have, or have not had. Our fight was to have—a territory under construction *(laughs)*. That was our fight. But even that territory for some of you younger people is already being under construction, and disciplined, if you will. And you pay for it if you want to get out of those tracks. So, I was fortunate in that sense. Especially as someone who wanted to be an intellectual and academic philosopher, a literary critic, whatever it was. I had a mentor that was very supportive of whatever it was because I was helping him with that construction. I was his graduate student, and he was a professor, but I was helping him with the construction. He had things of his own. He didn't care what I did as long as I was building, so to speak, using this metaphor. I think deconstructing and constructing will continue to be a constant struggle, but it may feel less of a struggle if you historicize that period of time. Take civil rights in the US context. If you historicize that period of time into the 21st century, you can also visualize how your struggle has changed. It is not the same as it was in the '70s, for me, or late '60s. It would not be the same any more. Even the language of the struggle would have changed. To keep in mind that it will continue to be a struggle, because the academy continues to be, and will continue to be, a patriarchal structure. Because it is the easiest thing it can be. It's its tradition.

**RR:** And a colonial structure.

**NA:** Yes, and it goes hand in hand with capitalism.

**RR:** It all goes together: the patriarchal structure, the colonial structure, the heterosexist structure—

**NA:** The political economy, with the academy thrown in to validate it. The academy validates the political economy. Maybe not the philosophy department in itself, but parts of the academy, too, in the way the philosophy department does help to maintain the tradition and to only push it just a little bit: guys that manifest on the one hand novelty and on the other the traditional patriarchal philosophy.

**RR:** From the level of assistant professors, we tend to think that things are getting easier when ascending the hierarchy of academy, but that's not necessarily the case. Binaries and hierarchies are not easy. Those who live a culture of resistance and maintain its memory will be regarded as a non-existing place in the traditional academy. Right now, I am in the beautiful situation to be in a place where I feel encouraged to construct, so in a certain sense what you just said, Norma, echoed in me. Academic careers are at times imagined as linear processes; you go and go and all of a sudden you "have" all the power. But this is really very relative. And also, do we want to be in and construct these imagined places where "all power" is? I don't think so, at least I would rather not.

**MB:** Sonia wants to say something.

**Sonia Saldívar-Hull:** When we do, we construct something outside of that condition you described. We have been trying to build a women's studies department here at the University of Texas at San Antonio. It is a very liberating project in some ways. But I am contracted as an English professor. When the women's studies working group included questions of race and class next to the masculine and feminine, we were constructing something new. By now we exist as a new women-of-color decolonial women's studies program, a victory indeed, but we have no money. We pay the cost with our invisible labor. It's heteropatriarchal capitalism. There is a price to pay: over-work, depression, PTSD, and so on.

**MB:** That's pointing to the next point of power, where we talk with Anzaldúa about the psychopathies of our creative life. Which aspects of your life do you exclude or marginalize? Which power struggles do you engage in? What are you paying for? From here, we do question pathologies. We engage in other questions, but all of a sudden, pathologies pop up again. It is like an iceberg. What makes us sick? But I also wanted to hear the audience—Laura, Sonia—about what Norma said and about life in the classroom in the many years of experience you have.

**RR:** So many voices present…las y los estudiantes aquí, what do you think?

**MB:** Irene, Sara, Elvia—and María, we heard already what you said this morning in your keynote—

**LP:** Irene and I were walking over with a young student that is now a healer in Berkeley. And we were talking about healing and how we need it, and how Berkeley needs it, and how ethnic studies needs it. The note that we ended on was on what happens in the classrooms. The student was complimenting the space she has had, the space Irene is creating. I don't know about others, but I do know that a lot of my energy in creativity has gone into rethinking the space of the classroom. I had to give myself a lot of permission. It's been an act of practice. It's been the creation and inhabitation of, in Norma's words, an interstitial space. To be able to think and enact a gap where we can acknowledge and provide the language for what *we* think is real, of what we think is interesting. All of us, including the faculty, experience this continual denial; the violence of continual appropriation and public degradation of the work. I find it really difficult to imagine a space that is rich, where all we do is lecture. I personally have always found this really difficult to take, I get very ADHD. I also think there is something about the politics of how we teach and how it is that we are treating the other: whether we are treating them as a receptacle, whether we treat ourselves as the ones who want to perform as the one in power. For me, it has been very healing to teach another point of view.

**Josie Méndez-Negrete:** I am having a conversation with myself. It begins with notions of pathologies of whatever type. The reason for that is, as a sociologist I always see it as a binary that locks you into a structural argument whereby the pathologies become individual practices, possessions, emotions. In reality, we need to look at the structure or the systemic quality. That is, how to be able to understand how in the academy we can make a difference and direct people to take ownership of the knowledge they engage with. The presupposition for me always is that students bring knowledge into my classroom, and that it increases the knowledge base for all of us—especially for me—because I may be able to unpack things that they have not yet seen, because they have not done what Norma did, to step outside and to see how the structure is limiting. The way I see it is that this has been a good place for us because Norma is here.

**MB:** Norma, a question that is at the tip of my tongue: What kind of power struggles did you engage with, were you arrasada por ellas?

**NA:** Let's see. My colleagues thought I was Eurocentric, that I was using European texts. Not all my texts were European. Okay, here is the contradiction, really: just because we want to undo patriarchy doesn't mean we want to throw all of it out.

**MB:** What do we want to keep?

**NA:** For myself, I thought I had to learn a sense of order that I could then throw out. Aristotle is all about methodology and method. So how do you throw it out? You can't throw out what you don't know. What is dysfunctional about patriarchy that I would throw out? We can't get away from knowing something about patriarchy because we are imprinted from the time we are born. Mom and Dad can't do it all. No matter how hard they try because there is also the television and other media doing it. The question is, how do you enable someone to throw it out? How can a person enable herself to throw it out?

**SSH:** I think you, Norma, and other women-of-color intellectuals have enabled some of us to throw it out. I don't need to go to Aristotle to engage a methodology. Sara Ramírez teaches our methodology Women's Studies courses. Where do you go *(asking Sara Ramírez)*?

**Sara Ramírez:** I go to Anzaldúa. The research class is a space where I "decolonize" the classroom space. We are no longer using Eurocentric conceptualizations of methodology, epistemology, ontology, which tell us who is human and what knowledge can be valued. So, I do ask students, for instance, in the very beginning of the class: Can plants tell you their properties? And they laugh, "Of course plants don't talk!" Then eventually we get into ontology and epistemology, which allow them to understand the different values we assign to what we believe to be living and non-living. And at the very end of the class they understand, "Oh, plants *can* speak to us. Alright, we have to consider non-Eurocentric epistemologies." I go to Anzaldúa, to Shawn Wilson, another indigenous scholar, Linda T. Smith, and scholars who have been influenced by others, like Aristotle. There is a history behind our methodologies. In my dissertation, I consult European philosophers. I bring them together. But I sometimes question why I have to do that.

**NA:** When I learn about Buddhism, I feel a deep existentialism of inner being. But I also like to read the existentialism as the Europeans do it. When a speaker conjugates Buddhist philosophy and existentialist philosophy, I am ecstatic. I am happy. I like conjugations. It could be a generational thing. I grew up adoring some philosophers, and I am not going to give them up for Gloria.

**LP:** Not even did Gloria herself.

**NA:** She didn't. I ran into Kierkegaard in her archives, and I said, "Ha, so you have been reading Kierkegaard!"

**JMN:** She read Sartre. She read a lot, to understand them and refute them, and to provide an alternative.

**NA:** She is reading Kierkegaard, and she is trying to understand herself. But anyway, that's what I mean by—no, I don't know what I mean about whatever. I am just telling you what gives me pleasure.

**SSH:** Pleasure?

**MB:** What gives you pleasure, Sonia?

**SSH:** Rejecting the patriarchs. See, I am feeling ecstatic right now *(Laughs, and laughter in the audience).*

**NA:** I do reject patriarchy's structures. But I still like the male body. Sorry. *(Laughs, and laughter in the audience)* The young one. (*Laughs, and more laughter in the audience*)

**LP:** I think that's very classic, like in the classical world. *(Laughter in the audience)*

**NA:** *(laughs)* Very Greek! *(Laughter in the audience)*

**María Lugones:** The old women in the codices were all into bodies, the young ones.

**Audience members:** *(intrigued)* Oh, I haven't seen that! Which codices?!

**ML:** In these long poems that the Europeans translated—

**NA:** In the Aztec codices?

**ML:** Yes. I also I wanted to say that I like if students show a sense of history, a sense that is not necessarily activated and that has to do with society. Right now, we have the Black Lives Matter movement. There is a sense of solidarity. In history, we decided to have women of color. As we are doing that, we are connecting directly to the classroom. The classroom is not just in there, in the edifices, it is also out there, it is where we are thinking, in the rebellion against the discourse, pushing against the disciplines. I was feeling small.

**NA:** Why small?

**ML:** The academy has always made me feel small.

**MB:** We can relate to that.

**LP:** I just want to say something really quickly. I want to acknowledge and emphasize one of the things you said, Norma. It is also about you, too, María. I think historically, and in the flesh, it is incredibly important to be women thinkers. Women thinkers, everywhere I have looked, have always existed, in different cultures, in different times. And it is incredibly difficult to be that. Norma made a distinction between what it means to be an academic. Would an academic's work be called "intellectual"? I really appreciate the distinction you have made. I think what it means to be an intellectual is something very creative, something very individual, without being individualist. It has to do with what is our destiny, with what is our path.

**ML:** As I engage with people in the disciplinary construction, es como una cosa que se te mete. Son bichos…

**NA:** What I learned in the struggle, being in Berkeley, was the rhetoric of a person in the disciplines. So I did. I *did* do that. But I did not *do* it in my work. But I had to, because you are listening to your overwhelmingly powerful colleagues. I am not talking ethnic studies any more either, although that was another vocabulary, oh my god. Anyway! *(Laughs)* So it was at the interstices of the powerful academy and ethnic studies, which had its own power. Those interstices: that would be my disciplinary location of a certain period of my life. That interstice. Both ethnic studies and the academy make you feel small, inconsequentially, and so on and so forth. But one of my methodological problems has been anger and rage.

**MB:** One of mine also.

**NA:** I think if you possess those things, perhaps you want to let them go onto your colleagues, so to speak, or you want to channel them into your work. And I can tell you that my work has been channelled by rage and anger. I recommend them if you know how to control them.

**SR:** Audre Lorde discusses rage and anger in her essay, "The Uses of Anger: Women Responding to Racism," in *Sister Outsider*.

**MB:** Right… Now, Norma, how do you translate that anger and rage?

**NA:** The strategy is to control it. It is like having a rope. Una reata, in Spanish. It can go out of control. And that's okay when you are being creative at the desk. Like Gloria talked about it, with the hand, the creativity of the intellectual life. But you know, Laura Pérez comes to my door, and I have to tell her, "Hey, Manita. Let's have un calmante, first, before we talk." *(Laughs, and laughter from the audience)* Because I am in a rage right now. And then you acknowledge that you are in a rage. But you are not afraid of it, and it's all yours. See, I am not trying to be a docent in rage. I am saying: I already had it. I am asking you: do you already have it? And what are you gonna do with it? And this is what I would say to you, María. And this is a way not to feel small.

**ML:** No. Small also in the sense how you were thinking about it.

**NA:** Oh! Well, this is all rage theory. *(Laughs, and laughter in the audience)*

**ML:** In my case, I think going with people to build spaces even if they don't last very long. My rage goes in them, and it makes me happier.

**NA:** Happier?

**ML:** Yes, happier.

**NA:** Well, it's intellectual pleasure. It is also a fulfilment of desire. Not sex, directly.

**MB:** Desire under construction…

**RR:** In Norma's words, to conjugate pleasure, anger, and power, inside and outside the classroom.

**SR:** Well, on *that* note… *(Laughter in the audience)* We have run out of time for this round table. Thank you so much for this great discussion.

## NOTES

1. This account was transcribed by Marisa Belausteguigoitia and Romana Radlwimmer and edited by Sara A. Ramírez. Speakers, other than those listed as authors, gave their permission to have their words included and verified the content of their comments.

2. Reagon, Bernice Johnson. "Coalition Politics: Turning the Century." *Home Girls: A Black Feminist Anthology*, edited by Barbara Smith, Rutgers UP, 2000, pp. 343–55. First published in 1983 by Kitchen Table Press.

3. Radlwimmer explains: "The Bologna Process is the restructuring of European higher education launched especially in the first decade of the new millennium. Advantages are, for instance, an easier transfer in studies and creditability of study results between the universities of different European countries. Study and internship programs abroad (such as ERASMUS) have become more easily accessible. Critiques of the reform of European higher education aim at the economization of education and the administrative predominance over critically open thinking structures."

4. "Meter caña" means "to fight with determination."

5. Alarcón, Norma: "Cognitive Desires: An Allegory of/for Chicana Critics." *Chicana (W) rites on Word and Film*, edited by María Herrera-Sobek and Helena María Viramontes, Third Woman Press, 1995, pp. 185–200: 186.

6. Alarcón, Norma: "The Theoretical Subject(s) of This Bridge Called My Back and Anglo-American Feminism." [1990] *Feminist Theory Reader: Local and Global Perspectives*, edited by Carole R. McCann and Seung-Kyung Kim, Taylor & Francis Books, 2003, pp. 404–414: 404.

7. Josie Méndez-Negrete discusses her son's struggle with mental illness in *A Life on Hold: Living with Schizophrenia*, U of New Mexico P, 2015.

8. Anzaldua, Gloria. "The New Mestiza Nation." *The Gloria Anzaldúa Reader*, edited by AnaLouise Keating, Duke UP, 2009, pp. 203–216: 212.

# (RE)VIEWING & (RE)MEMBERING VIOLENCE

## TESTIMONIOS OF QUEER AND TRANS TEJAN@X SEXUAL ASSAULT EXPERIENCES

RICHARD GIDDENS, JR.

You turn the established narrative on its head, seeing through, resisting, and subverting its assumptions. Again, it's not enough to denounce the culture's old account—you must provide new narratives that embody alternative potentials. You're sure of one thing: the consciousness that's created our social ills (dualistic and misogynist) cannot solve them—we need a more expansive *conocimiento*: "The new stories must partially come from outside the system of ruling powers" (Anzaldúa, "now let us shift" 140).

### WHY THIS STUDY IS IMPORTANT FOR MY COMMUNITY

According to statistics provided by the US Census and Gallup.com, approximately 35,016 people in the San Antonio/New Braunfels metroplex identify as queer and/or transgender Latin@x people.[1] A large majority of these Latin@x San Antonians are of Mexican descent. Queer and trans Tejan@x people living in San Antonio, Texas who have been sexually assaulted have little to no available resources for collective group healing tailored to the needs of Tejan@x people. I know this because I personally needed these resources and have done the research only to find a single group program provided by the San Antonio Rape Crisis Center. The website of the San Antonio Rape Crisis Center, where one would go to find these resources, is questionable in regard to whom this resource is meant to serve. Though the site boasts in its heading, "Serving Children, Women, and Men," it isn't as obvious about the inclusion of queer, transgender, and gender non-binary people as those also invited to partake in this particular source of healing.

One would have to scroll down six pages at rapecrisis.com to find, at the very end of the San Antonio Rape Crisis Center's homepage, a small "tacked-on" bit of information that reads, "SAFE ZONE: This space respects all aspects of people including race, ethnicity, gender expression, sexual orientation, income level, age, religion, body shape, size and ability." Granted, this information is present, but the missed opportunity by not including this disclaimer earlier in the website's topography could be preventing a queer and/or trans or gender non-binary person of color from acquiring these dire services. A critique can also be made about how the lack of dark-skinned representation on this resource's homepage leaves one with an air of colorism. Right now in San Antonio, Tejan@x people have no access to an exclusive formal or informal discussion group to facilitate communal healing. This lack of support is a direct result of the underreporting of these assaults. Yet institutionalized cis-heteronormativity creates the conditions for underreporting, lack of sexual assault resources, and education that is not inclusive of queer and trans people in San Antonio.

This study aims to understand the ways that Tejan@x people navigate healing while continuing to contend with sexual violence supported and enforced by cis-heteropatriarchy. In this study I refer to participants as "co-researchers"[2] to understand how they navigate what queer Chicana feminist Gloria Anzaldúa terms "nepantla," or the in-between space that queer people of color exist in as it pertains to the socially prescribed identity of the "rape victim/survivor."[3] Drawing from Anzaldúan feminist thought, this study also aims to understand how co-researchers (re)view and (re)member to make sense of how they (we) cope and heal from this trauma. Anzaldúa reminds us that in (re)membering the trauma, those who experience trauma are able to gain new awareness of their experiences and piece back together parts of their fractured identities into one whole fluid unit or member—a process she explains as the Coyolxauhqui imperative. She writes, "The Coyolxauhqui imperative is an ongoing process of making and unmaking. There is never any resolution, just the process of healing" ("Let us be the healing" 20). This research is just this, the putting back together of all the participants' identities as a method of healing from trauma that is anchored in cis-heteropatriarchy. In "Speaking across the Divide," Anzaldúa explains,

> the path of the artist, the creative impulse, what I call the Coyolxauhqui imperative is basically an attempt to heal the wounds. It's a search for inner completeness. Suffering is one of the motivating forces of the creative impulse. Adversity calls forth your best energies and most creative solutions. (292)

This research is the result of suffering and adversity that has called forth the best energies in my co-researchers and me to heal ourselves by creating counter-narratives critiquing state-sponsored healing resources after experiencing sexual assault. These narratives are largely nonexistent in academia.

In this work, I postulate that institutionalized cis-heteronormativity and rape culture work together to silence these forms of violence and work against the assaulted by inducing self-hate and self-shame in them, which, in turn, prevents them from reporting the assault and seeking immediate physical and mental medical attention. The shame, silence, and denial of sexual violence experienced by queer and trans Tejan@x then prevents their long-term psychological healing. I also argue that, because of the shaming enforced by institutionalized cis-heteronormativity paired with rape culture, there are not many, if any, exclusively Tejan@x sexual assault support groups for the assaulted to access. Because the sexual assault survivor resources currently present are highly tailored to the experiences of cisgender heterosexual women, I did not recruit cisgender heterosexual men or women who have been sexually assaulted to participate. My focus is specifically on queer and/or trans people.

The literature currently produced in the studies of cis-heterosexual violence and trauma is abundant, yet the literature currently produced in the studies of queer and trans people of color's experiences of sexual violence and trauma is desolate. The necessity of an intersectional methodology is core to this decolonial research endeavor, because, as queer and trans black/brown bodies, we experience multiple forms of oppression, including the non-inclusion and erasure of our experiences, that come from all angles of life: our peers as children and adults, families, cultures, and the world in which our institutions facilitate and perpetuate white supremacy and cis-heteropatriarchy. When studying a specific culture, in my case the queer and trans Tejan@x community, the current literature does not bolster much. We are multifaceted and subject to multiple oppressions, one of these being the silencing of our plight, and the literature reflects this.

By recording, analyzing, and sharing these testimonios, a wealth of knowledge will be available to scholars and academics, not to mention social workers and other practitioners who will be able to rely on this research to inform new perspectives, methods, and pedagogies concerning the psychological and spiritual healing of Tejan@x people who have experienced sexual assault.

## WHAT OTHER SCHOLARS HAVE WRITTEN

The Centers for Disease Control reports that "an estimated 19.3% of women and 1.7% of men have been raped during their lifetimes" (Breiding 7). This statistic is problematic because it conforms to a gender binary of man or woman, and some queer and/or trans people do not. Here we have an example of the erasure or non-inclusion of the queer and/or trans experience. According to the Human Rights Campaign (HRC), 44% of lesbians and 61% of bisexual women experience rape, physical violence, or stalking by an intimate partner, compared to 29% of heterosexual women; 26% of gay men and 37% of bisexual men compared to 29% of heterosexual men; 46% of bisexual women have been raped, compared to 17% of heterosexual women and 13% of lesbians; 40% of gay men and 47% of bisexual men have experienced sexual violence other than rape compared to 27% of heterosexual men. In each of these comparisons it is clear that of the reported assaults, the majority are experienced by the LGBTQIA+ community. The HRC also reports, "85 percent of victim advocates surveyed by the National Coalition of Anti-Violence Programs (NCAVP) reported having worked with an LGBTQIA+ survivor who was denied services because of their sexual orientation or gender identity." The National Transgender Discrimination Survey found that among those transgender respondents who had interacted with police, 6% had been physically assaulted and 2% had been sexually assaulted by police. Among black transgender people, 15% reported physical assault and 7% reported sexual assault by police. Additionally, 22% of those transgender people who had attempted to access shelters reported being sexually assaulted by either another person in the shelter or by shelter staff. This is a very real situation in shelters in the US serving queer and trans homeless youth. An analysis of this literature shows that queer and/or trans Tejan@x people are more likely to experience sexual assault than cisgender and/or heterosexual men and women. This study aims to understand the ways that Tejan@x folks navigate healing while continuing to contend with sexual violence supported and enforced by cis-heteropatriarchy. Some patterns and themes that emerged in the literature include the comparison of experiencing child sexual assault and the development of a non-heterosexual orientation later in life; the comparison of experiencing child sexual assault and the likelihood of being re-victimized as an adult; debunking the causal comparison of childhood sexual assault and sexual orientation development; queer hegemony and discrimination against queer people of color; queer intimate partner violence and institutionalized trans discrimination within domestic violence resources, rape crisis centers, and shelters.

## HOW WE DID IT, AND WHY WE DID IT THIS WAY: TESTIMONIO AS COUNTERNARRATIVE

The high reflexivity of my subject position as both a researcher and a Tejan@ person who has experienced sexual assault is at the core of this methodology. There is plenty of quantitative data to sort through in an attempt to discover the answers to questions we may have about sexual assault and the LGBTQIA+ community, but testimonios as a method are the gateway to the required alternative ways of knowing.[4] Testimonios are the life-preservers that give marginalized and erased experiences a second chance to be heard and validated. As a starting point, the sample goal of this project is the collection of testimonios respectively borrowed from a group of Tejan@x people. I've conducted one-on-one interviews/testimonios with each of my "co-researchers," a term borrowed from Shawn Wilson's *Research Is Ceremony* in which he discusses how an indigenous research paradigm calls for full disclosure and participation between the researcher and co-researchers in order to create a shared communal knowledge that can improve the lives of the community in question (10). Full disclosure and inclusivity of all participants in the creation of this study is a key component of the indigenous research paradigm that this research adheres to, and, in doing so, it decolonizes mainstream academic research methods that keep the research subject separate from the research plan and analysis. This work reflects my existence as a queer Tejan@ nepantler@ and is heavily centered around healing through the power of personal narrative, performance, and the production of what Chicana literary and cultural critics have termed "theory in the flesh," or as Cherríe Moraga and Gloria Anzaldúa proclaim, "a theory in the flesh means one where the physical realities of our lives—our skin color, the land or concrete we grew up on, our sexual longings—all fuse to create a politic born out of necessity" (23). Following an indigenous research paradigm and a US Third World feminist theoretical framework, I approach this project with a decolonial mindset that requires transparency and validation of the lived experience of my co-researchers. The use of an indigenous research paradigm will further the production of communal knowledge that will benefit the San Antonio LGBTQIA+ community.

## TEJAN@X TESTIMONIO

The most common experience, shared by all co-researchers thus far, is that immediately after our assaults occurred, we each blamed ourselves for the event. Conversely, later in life we were able to dismiss self-blame, resulting in a new self-awareness, and ultimately the process of unlearning was salubrious for each of us. The three co-researchers and I all experienced self-blame, but I was the only person who reported my assault to the police. The fact that no one else reported to the police seems to be mostly due to a fear of law enforcement and/or internalized shame and self-blame, and may also have to do with the three co-researchers all experiencing assaults that occurred in childhood; I did not. With my many social privileges being a man with light skin, I convinced myself that reporting my assault would be the right thing to do, and perhaps even beneficial to my recovery. Privilege has a way of blinding those it benefits. As it turns out, the reasons given by my three co-researchers for not calling the police or seeking medical attention were almost exact descriptions of how I was treated when I sought help the evening after I was assaulted.

### MI TESTIMONIO

I approached the front desk clerk at the Medical Center University Hospital Emergency Room, who just stared at me with a blank look on her face, waiting for me to say something, but I couldn't, I couldn't utter the words. So I took a piece of paper from the top of her desk and a pen from her pen repository, and wrote down why I was there: three words, *I was raped*. Her blank look went quickly from blank-old-white-woman to disgusted-old-white-woman. The next thing out of her mouth, I know now, was entirely fabricated, "Are you sure you want to do this, because we are required to call the police when these things happen." I suppose I'd already weighed out the pros and cons, and I, as a documented/white-passing/cisgender man with little to no reason to fear the police, said, "Sure, call them." It turned out that all she did was call the police, and as I gave a mortifying explanation of my assault to the officer, conducted not in a triage or meeting room or even a nurse's cubicle, but in the overfilled ER waiting room, my assault narrative became that evening's entertainment for those present. The punch line was two-fold. I now know that by law, people who seek medical attention after being sexually assaulted have a no-report option that doesn't involve the police in any way. It is only mandatory to call the police if the person seeking help is under the age of eighteen; the final slap in the face was the officer escorting me to my car so that I could follow him to Methodist Hospital down the street, because the front desk woman failed to inform me that University Hospital doesn't even provide rape kits. Because I am a man who chose to report my assault (going against the normative silence that most men who experience sexual assault keep secret) my entire experience in the University Hospital emergency room was made up of disidentificatory performances. From the initial explanation of my reason for seeking care, to the police escort out of the crowded waiting area. These performances, though traumatic, were one hundred percent politically charged and can be understood as what José Esteban Muñoz calls "disidentifications"; his theory is built upon the multiple theorizations of the *identity-in-difference* concept, theorized by US Third World feminists Anzaldúa, Moraga, Chela Sandoval, Norma Alarcón, and Audre Lorde, along with Jacques Derrida. Muñoz explains disidentificatory performance:

> The disidentificatory identity performances I catalog in these pages are all emergent identities-in-difference. These identities-in-difference emerge from a failed interpellation within the dominant public sphere. Their emergence is predicated on their ability to disidentify with the mass public and instead, through this disidentification, contribute to the function of a counterpublic sphere. (7)

As a cisgender queer man, I certainly did not fit the dominant narrative of who should be seeking medical care after being sexually assaulted. The front desk nurse made that obviously clear, but I was determined to have my experience heard and my body cared for with antibiotics and my psyche evaluated by someone who would take my assault seriously, no matter how chagrinned I may have felt.

## NEMAMAUHTILO

As decolonial researchers working with "human subjects," we sometimes witness the raw power of testimonio, especially when researching trauma. As trauma sufferers, we each heal in our own time and in our own ways; there is no one definitive method. Throughout the undertaking of this research, one of my co-researcher-subject(s)-in-process decided to rescind their testimonio unexpectedly. Keeping with my core decolonial framework, I had no problems removing all identifiable traces of them from this project. Their experiences were some of the most horrendous events I've ever heard. I've titled this section "Nemamauhtilo," which is Nahuatl, meaning "there is constant fear." The process of transcribing their testimonio was difficult, to say the least, and the overall theme I collected was one of general fear, and a furious virginitiphobia: the morbid fear of being sexually assaulted. We must understand that when we ask for a glimpse into another's trauma, profound care must be taken. Even when we feel we have been entirely considerate of others' stories, the trauma located within, once projected outward into the light, can bring upon new anxieties and concerns. When this co-researcher informed me that they no longer wished to be a part of the project, my first instinct was to think that I had somehow made them feel unsafe: Where did I go wrong? How had I failed to create a space where they could feel comfortable? Perhaps I was too inviting and forthcoming creating an air of expropriation between us. These questions still rest in the back of my mind, but in the end, I must learn from this experience, and wish them love, health, and well-being on their journey.

### XOCHITL

My second co-researcher-subject-in-process, who chose to be identified as the Nahuatl word for flower, Xochitl, identifies as a Queer/Cisgender/Bisexual/Femme/(Un)documented/(Im)migrant/Radical/Xican@/Tejan@/Woman/PhD Student who is openly queer to her friends but still closets her sexuality from her parents' view at age twenty-two. For our data-collection session, Xochitl met me at her friend's residence in the early evening. We were given access to one of the bedrooms and we locked ourselves in, figuratively. With Chicano Batman playing softly in the background, I shared my testimonio with the co-researcher. This was the second time I shared my experience with sexual assault for this project, and the second time sharing, period. In retrospect, this process proved cathartic; I can tell in the audio that I'm a lot more comfortable talking about my trauma.

Xochitl's experiences differed from mine and revealed my own privilege in comparison. For instance, the concept of privilege came up in our session many times, always acknowledging our specific privileges that make us less aware of the plight of the further marginalized. Also, when Xochitl was a child living in Mexico, her father worked in aviation, so her family wasn't poor in relation to the extreme poverty of Mexico, which seems to have inspired guilt in Xochitl about her relatively harmless transnational journey to the US when a post-9/11 aviation opportunity presented itself for her father. Xochitl was also one of the group who didn't trust law enforcement officers, and this she explained when I asked, "When did the cops become scary?" Xochitl responded:

> …for me, I can think about specifically the day. I was ten, eleven, or twelve? I was probably twelve. No, I was little 'cause I hadn't started middle school, and we still lived in the apartments; I was probably like nine or eight, and uhm, a cop and ICE came to our house to deport my

> dad, and my sister and I had just gotten out of the shower. We were like in towels, well she was naked, and they came into our room. And they saw my sister naked, and they saw me in a towel sitting there...and then I remember he had a badge. They were wearing normal clothes, but he had a badge, and ever since then I was like, I'm never going to trust men with badges. That's why cops always scare me...like my parents don't call the cops.

She also added that there is no way she could ever tell her parents she was queer, because they would disown her. Xochitl was a child the first time she was sexually assaulted at the hands of the most popular guy at school, when she was about thirteen years old. She then went on to say that because of her assault experiences she "thought sex was supposed to be that way." This violent misinformation, she believes, is to blame for a relationship she had in her later teen years with an older adult man in her neighborhood, a man who would allow Xochitl to come over almost daily to be sexually assaulted. It wasn't until her present age of twenty-two, after taking a women's studies course in college, that she realized she'd been the prey of many men almost her entire life. She also confessed that this testimonio was the first and only time she spoke about the many incidents in which she was in great danger of being murdered, and her reason for this was because when she was going through all this in her teen years, she would regularly come down with a UTI, and when her mother noticed this, Xochitl was chastised.

For self-care and self-love, Xochitl paints, is highly involved with undocumented queer people-of-color social justice movements, has a very active sex life, and medicinally consumes cannabis. It is through these methods of validation that she is able to (re)generate herself as one of many *nepantleras* striving for social change. Her specific subject-position as an undocumented queer gives a certain clout and validation to others who may or even may not know a similar struggle. It is through the validation and empowerment of our differences that we are able to bond together in the fight against a white supremacist, cis-heteronormative, capitalist patriarchy.

### MANZANA

My third co-researcher-subject-in-process, who will be referred to as the Spanish word for apple, Manzana, is in his late forties, making him the eldest co-researcher. We met at his apartment in central San Antonio—a humble, one-bedroom loft. Manzana explained he came from a middle-class, military family background that may suggest he was raised with a level of financial stability and middle-class privilege. He lives his life as a proud effeminate gay man, drag performer, and staunch Catholic. Manzana was raised by his grandfather. I listened to Manzana explain how he was threatened with violence by his grandfather if he were ever to be physically violent towards a woman. Manzana described his relationship with his grandfather proudly; "he raised us to be the best." By "the best," he seems to mean he was raised to not disrespect women, and also taught how a "real man" should and shouldn't behave. This suggests that Manzana was indoctrinated with a masculine gender prescription, like most boys are, and this suggestion becomes more apparent when he explains that he wasn't feminine as a child. In regard to his self-care in the form of awareness and assurance of self, he admitted it wasn't until he was in his thirties that he understood he was not to blame for being assaulted. Manzana went on to say that as a child he never saw himself as queer, and only in adulthood did he come to identify as a gay Hispanic man.

Next, we focused on the experience and survival of sexual assault. When asked how the assault affected his self-worth he responded with, "well, to me, it was like we were taught to believe it [the assault] was right...that it was ok... that there was nothing wrong, but...inside of us we knew it was wrong because the way we were raised...but still, you know, I ended up liking it." This portion of Manzana's testimonio paints a picture of a confused boy torn between what knowledge he was taught as a child through formal religion and education, and his *conocimiento* developed by his personal experience. I know from personal experience, and professional expertise, that sexual exploration is not uncommon among children. As early as five years old I knew I was attracted to men, and as early as nine I started exploring my sexuality with other boys my own age. Manzana never searched for healing resources, and had only discussed his assaults with his first lover prior to this project. When asked generally about his experiences of being a gay man searching for public resources, he spoke about the queer experience in the ER:

> I mean sometimes, you know, like when you go to the doctors, like ERs and stuff like they wear like all kinds of stuff, like they ask you, you know, if you're, you know, you're gay or are you straight, you know or whatever. They go down the line, like then they go on, they go, are you HIV or whatever, you know so you go, you say no, but they still take their precautions, and they like look at you all freaky, gloves on.

Manzana's experiences with doctors and hospitals are filled with homophobia, and stigma related to HIV in the queer community.

For self-care and self-love, Manzana performs in drag shows and in theater productions. As a young Tejan@x, he metamorphosed the stress incurred by the assaults and cathartically transferred it into action. Consciously creating a performance and, as he stated, "shining more when shining to heal," he also started doing drag performances when his grandfather died. He made it a point to mention that his performances as Selena Quintanilla-Perez, beginning in 1992, have proven to be most salubrious: his first disidentification, being that the performance was one symbolically owned by mainstream hetero Tejano culture, was the song "Las Cadenas," by the late Selena. When queering the lyrics to this song and connecting them to Manzana's debut drag performance, "Las Cadenas," or "The Chains," as it translates to English, is a ballad of liberation and healing through self-care and self-love through which Manzana broke free of the patriarchal cadenas machistas that had imprisoned him since childhood. It isn't to be overlooked that Manzana didn't begin performing in drag until his grandfather passed away, and the lyrics to "Las Cadenas" serve as an example of Manzana's disidentificatory liberation through taboo mainstream as well as taboo Tejano cultural performance. This queer liberation by my co-researcher-subject-in-process through his disidentificatory performance can be understood as resistance to the cadenas/chains of racist cis-heteronormativity. Through performance, Manzana lifts and unlocks these chains and makes his way on a path of sexual assault survival.

From each of my co-researcher-subject(s)-in-process(es), including myself, I've collected similar, yet vastly different experiences of survival. Each of us has taken our healing into our own hands through many different forms of disidentificatory artistic expression. We are healers, painters, drag performers, social justice activists, academics, poets, volunteers, queer, transgender, cisgender, women, men, human beings, and we are living day-to-day with our trauma. We practice self-care and self-love in a world that tells us we are undeserving of care and love. We heal in ways that are unique to our circumstances, with the assistance of our fellow queer and/or trans people, our jotería, and chosen familia.

## NEW CONOCIMIENTOS

It has become apparent that sexual violence is an offense that Tejan@x people in said recovery do, in fact, navigate with more obstacles than average. The ways that my co-researchers navigate their individual survivals are each unique, yet equally structured involving a creative component. This is what makes each of us a co-researcher-subject-in-process utitilizing disidentificatory performance, through our own preferred mode of creativity as well as the testimonios given for this project as methods of healing (self-care, self-love). It has also been made evident that there is a shared fear and distrust of law enforcement among those Tejan@x people who are currently dealing with sexual assault trauma, causing them to not report their assaults out of fear of retaliation by institutionalized cis-heteronormativity within the police and law enforcement industrial complex as well as in the current state of sexual assault resources, behavioral and medical healthcare services in San Antonio. I suspect this discrimination is also evident in other queer and transgender communities of color across the United States. After doing this work, I have learned that Tejan@x people living with sexual assault trauma are certainly contending with cis-heteronormative roadblocks to healing, which are therefore necessarily battled with new ways of navigating said healing through cultural expression exclusive to Tejan@x culture.

As you can see from the testimonios shared by my co-researcher-subject(s)-in-process(es) and our disidentificatory modes of cathartic artistic expression—with mine ultimately being this project—we do, in fact, create ways to self-care and ways to resist dominant cis-heteronormative power structures that do not include us or welcome us to be a part of the mainstream state of sexual assault healing resources, as I suspected. I also learned that the methods and theories created by Gloria Anzaldúa, Norma Alarcón, Cherríe Moraga, José

Esteban Muñoz, Juana María Rodríguez, and Shawn Wilson, when combined, have to the power to decolonize; (de)/(re)construct; and shed light upon the continued marginalization of, and give validation of self to, Tejan@x people living in sexual assault survival. This work teaches us that much is to be done in order to create a system of sexual assault resources that will be beneficial to more than just an archetypical cis-heternormative representation of who a person living with sexual assault trauma should be, and is.

## CODA: HEALING FROM THE WORK

To write is to confront one's demons, look them in the face and live to write about them. Fear acts like a magnet; it draws the demons out of the closet and into the ink in our pens:

> *Write with your eyes like painters, with your ears like musicians, with your feet like dancers. You are the truthsayer with quill and torch. Write with your tongues of fire. Don't let the pen banish you from yourself. Don't let the ink coagulate in your pens. Don't let the censor snuff out the spark, nor the gags muffle your voice. Put your shit on the paper.* (Anzaldúa, "Speaking In Tongues" 173)

The past year I have spent constructing this research, telling and retelling my own personal experience with sexual assault trauma, has been a year of shock, pain, exhaustion, fear, addiction, desperation, heartbreak, transformation, hope, recovery, and healing. To be perfectly honest, I didn't know what I was getting myself into when I began this journey. Armed with a background in US Third World Feminist Theory, and supported by my mentors, Jackie Cuevas, Sonia Saldívar-Hull, Sara A. Ramírez, Lilliana Saldaña, Sonia Valencia, and Ben Olguín, I dove headfirst into a project that would ultimately consume and imprison me in my first Coatlicue State experience, from which I didn't think I'd ever escape.

This project consumed me. The research stole my sleep and my time for self-care. I was too busy preparing this research for this conference at UC Berkeley and that conference at UCLA, graduate school preparation, Cambridge application, Stanford application, Brown application, and the list went on and on. I lost myself, my mind, my soul, my marriage. Suddenly all I had worked for and toward was looking less and less tangible. I was in my first Coatlicue State, described by Anzaldúa:

> To escape emotional pain (most of it self-imposed), you indulge in addictions. These respites from reality allow you to feel at one with yourself and the world, gaining you brief sojourns in Tamoanchan (paradise). When you surface to the present, your unrelenting consciousness shrieks, "Stop resisting the truth of what's really happening, face your reality." But salvation is illusive, like the scent of a dim memory. De éste lugar de muerte viva the promise of sunlight is unreachable. Though you want deliverance, you cling to your misery. ("now let us shift" 129)

For me, the emotional pain I was going through was the trauma from my assault cropping up through the writing of this research; the unequal power dynamic in my marriage; the abandonment issues incurred from my parents' divorce, specifically in regard to the absence of a strong father-son relationship; as well as internalized racism and homophobia. Addiction was the easiest escape: allowing me to momentarily run away from these fears and damaging emotions. My unrelenting consciousness slapped me in the face when I realized that I no longer recognized the person looking at me in the mirror. I had to face my truth, what was really happening; my reality was that I needed help. In January of this year, the beginning of my final semester of my undergraduate career, I checked myself into a thirty-day in-residence rehabilitation facility, and soberly reassessed my life. This was the best decision I've ever made. I chose the facility I attended only because it offered a specific group therapy for people who identified as members of the LGBTQIA+ community, dubbed the Freedom Group. I've come to realize in recovery that there are no coincidences in life. I now know first-hand the benefits of a queer-specific resource of healing; and to this group and others, like my mentors who allowed me to begin my semester a month late, I owe my life. This research project began as a search for queer healing from sexual assault, and through the course of its fruition, my addiction brought me to the exact experience I was longing for. The proof is in the healing. The queer community in general, and Tejan@x people in particular, need these services. There is much more work to be done, and I'm grateful to be alive to spread this awareness. The salvation is indeed elusive, as Anzaldúa tells us, but through the decolonization of academia, social services, the LGBTQIA+ community, and our own desconocimientos, we can heal—only together, and never alone.

## NOTES

1. In Mexican American/Chicana/o, and Latina/o Studies, scholars and activists have summoned attention to the need for further theorizing gender through their use of new orthography, such as the "@" and "X" suffixes, as in "Latin@" and "Latinx." For the dialogue of this paper, "Latin@" denotes a sometimes-fluid gender identity embracing the feminine as well as masculine. Sandra Soto uses the @ in the title of her book, and explains, "I like the way the non alphabetic symbol for 'at' disrupts our desire for intelligibility, our desire for a quick and certain visual register of a gendered body the split second we see or hear the term" (2–3). The @ doesn't always signal gender fluidity; it is largely used to be inclusive of women when speaking about the overall Latinx community, since "LatinO" erases their presence. "Latinx" denotes the intended removal of a gender binary altogether for gender non-binary (GNB) and transgender identities that exist beyond a limiting cisgender male/female binary. Scholar-activist communities in Texas further theorized and adopted the @/x suffixes to describe the Texas-specific Chican@/Chicanx identities and thus use "Tejan@/Tejanx." I'd like to suggest the next form of an all-inclusive suffix alternative to Tejano, Chicano, and Latino could be the use of both the "@" and "X" suffixes together as one, as I use this suffix throughout this essay. While I use the suffixes together to create an all-inclusive neologism, I recognize we must individually choose our own suffixes and/or terms.

2. "Co-researchers" used to refer to study participants is a decolonial term borrowed from Shawn Wilson's *Research is Ceremony*. I use this term to deconstruct the researcher/research-subject power dynamic.

3. There exists feminist scholarship about rape, which discusses the implications of using the term "survivor" versus "victim" to empower people who have been raped. See Hocket, "A Systematic Literature Review of 'Rape Victims' Versus 'Rape Survivors': Implications for Theory, Research, and Practice."

4. For more on testimonio as a method, see *Telling to Live: Latina Feminist Testimonios* by The Latina Feminist Group.

## WORKS CITED


Anzaldúa, Gloria. "Let us be the healing of the wound: The Coyolxauhqui imperative—La sombra y el sueño." *Light in the Dark/Luz en lo Oscuro: Rewriting Identity, Spirituality, Reality*, edited by AnaLouise Keating, Duke UP, 2015, pp. 9–22.

---. "now let us shift…conocimiento…inner work, public acts." *Light in the Dark/Luz en lo Oscuro: Rewriting Identity, Spirituality, Reality*, edited by AnaLouise Keating, Duke UP, 2015, pp. 117–159.

---. "Speaking across the Divide." *The Gloria Anzaldúa Reader*, edited by AnaLouise Keating, Duke UP, 2009, pp. 282–94.

---. "Speaking in Tongues: A Letter to 3rd World Women Writers." *This Bridge Called My Back: Writings by Radical Women of Color*, edited by Cherríe Moraga and Gloria Anzaldúa, 2nd ed., Kitchen Table Press, 1983, pp. 165–174.

Breiding, Matthew J., Sharon G. Smith, Kathleen C. Basile, Mikel L. Walters, Jieru Chen, and Melissa T. Merrick. "Prevalence and Characteristics of Sexual Violence, Stalking, and Intimate Partner Violence Victimization—National Intimate Partner and Sexual Violence Survey, United States, 2011." *Surveillance Summaries*, vol 63, no. 8, 2014, pp. 1–22. http://www.cdc.gov/mmwr/pdf/ss/ss6308.pdf. Accessed 31 May 2016

Hocket, Jericho, and Donald Saucier. "A Systematic Literature Review of 'Rape Victims' Versus 'Rape Survivors': Implications for Theory, Research, and Practice." *Aggression and Violent Behavior*, vol 25, part A, 2015, pp. 1–14.

"Sexual Assault and the LGBTQ Community." *Human Rights Campaign*, http://www.hrc.org/resources/sexual-assault-and-the-lgbt-community. Accessed 31 May 31 2016.

Latina Feminist Group, editors. *Telling to Live: Latina Feminist Testimonios*. Duke UP, 2001.

Manzana. Personal Testimonio. 13 October 2016.

Moraga, Cherríe, and Gloria E. Anzaldúa, editors. *This Bridge Called My Back: Writings by Radical Women of Color*. 3rd ed. Third Woman Press, 2002.

Muñoz, José Esteban. *Disidentifications: Queers of Color and the Performance of Politics*. U of Minnesota P, 1999.

Grant, Jamie, Mottet, Lisa, and J.D. Justin Tanis. "National Transgender Discrimination Survey." *National Center for Transgender Equality*, http://www.transequality.org/sites/default/files/docs/resources/NTDS_Report.pdf. Accessed 31 May 2016.

Newport, Frank and Gary J. Gates. "San Francisco Metro Area Ranks Highest in LGBT Percentage." *GALLUP*, March 2015, http://www.gallup.com/poll/182051/san-francisco-metro-area-ranks-highest-lgbtpercentage.aspx. Accessed May 31, 2016.

Soto, Sandra K. *Reading Chican@ Like A Queer: The De-Mastery of Desire*. U of Texas P, 2010.

The Rape Crisis Center. "Homepage." *The Rape Crisis Center*, http://www.rapecrisis.com. Accessed 31 May 2016.

United States Census Bureau. "Quick Facts: San Antonio City, Texas." http://www.census.gov/quickfacts/table/PST045215/4865000,48029. Accessed 31 May 2016.

Wilson, Shawn. *Research is Ceremony: Indigenous Research Methods*. Fernwood Publishing, 2008.

Xochitl. Personal Testimonio. 22 August 2016.

# WELCOME TO THE AUSTRALIAN BORDERLANDS

## ENGAGING WITH THE TOLD EXPERIENCES OF REFUGEE-BACKGROUND YOUTH[1]

FABIANE RAMOS

### INTRODUCTION

It was a windy day. 2014. The trees outside my window were moving frantically. The wind blew in all directions. The trees outside my window looked confused. I felt confused. Moving in all directions, not knowing where to go… It was early in my PhD. Every day was a stormy day. I felt uneasy and confused about the expectations of a PhD. I also felt limited because I did not know how to express these emotions and thoughts. Trying to frame my questions about research into the theories I had been reading felt contrived. I, a mestiza, migrant, multilingual woman, felt a sense of exclusion and alienation when engaging with the theorists I was asked to read.

Then I met her, and after reading only a few words from *Borderlands/La Frontera*, I realized she had profound things to tell me. She spoke to me with a fierce yet loving voice that went straight to my heart-mind-soul. She opened up the possibility of theorizing through beautiful poetic texts. Elegant and sophisticated theorizing that spoke to me, that included me and the people who worked with me in my doctoral research project as thinking subjects. I met Gloria Anzaldúa on that windy day, and she gifted me with a language I wanted to speak.

In the following, I experiment with Anzaldúa's language as part of a doctoral project in which I engage with Borderlands theory (*Borderlands*, *Light in the Dark*, "On the Process of Writing *Borderlands*") to frame the complexities of being a young person of refugee background in Australia.[2] As I write, I hear Anzaldúa's voice like a soft breeze guiding me through every turn, lending words and concepts to my readings of told experiences. This letter—addressed to the seven people who shared their stories of migration with me—reveals the responses and interpretations I developed in relation to the stories of arrival and "re-settlement" in Australia.[3]

*

*My name is Naarin.*[4] *I'm actually from Kurdistan in Iran—the Iranian part, I'd say. Most people call us "Iranian" or call us "Kurdish." It really doesn't matter. I'm twenty-three turning twenty-four, and I have been here for like eleven years now. I decided to take part* [in this project] *because I think it would be a good insight for people to understand what other people go through and not just judge them or think you are not good enough, because we get that a lot, especially saying that you are from a refugee background.*

*

*My name is Faith, I am twenty years of age. I am from the Democratic Republic of Congo, and I arrived here in Australia in 2012. I'm currently studying a double degree of nursing and public health. I really wanted to share my story to encourage other youth, other students who are still in high school, that with education they can do many things.*

*

*I'm Jestor, and I'm a second-year university student, and I'm from Burma. I came here as a refugee due to conflict that was happening due to some political reasons. This is my fourth year in Australia, and I'm currently nineteen years old. I live with my parents and my brother and sister; we live together. My siblings are older than me. We all came here together in January 2011. I want to share my story because, you know, like coming from different background and country, they helped us so why not share, share my story with other people?*

*

*My name is Danny. I was born in Burundi, but I grew up in Tanzania in the refugee camp, and I came here in 2007, and I'm turning twenty this year. My whole family came here together—all my brothers and sisters and my parents. We are eight: four boys and four girls. I'm the second-youngest. I decided to share my story because I've never done this kind of thing, and I wanted to try to see how it feels. It would be nice to see if some people can relate to it and maybe learn something.*

*

*My name is Gabriela. I'm twenty-five years old. I was born in Burundi, which is in East Central Africa, maybe the second-smallest country in the world, I think. The population is huge but the country is so poor. Most of the families have three to six kids, so it's really hard. I've been here for about eight years; I arrived in 2007. I want to share my story because you said that you were doing your PhD, and I wanted to be part of your study. Sometimes sharing a story—it helps you to learn more about me or my culture or other people. I was just happy to help you. I know that from sharing stories people can find solutions for issues; probably now you understand part of where I'm coming from.*

*

*My name is Mary. I'm twenty years old, and I come from Burundi, but my grandmother is from Rwanda, so I have a bit of Rwandan heritage with me. We came to Australia in 2009, in April, from Zimbabwe. We lived in the Zimbabwean refugee camp before we were given the humanitarian visa by the United Nations to come to Australia. We lived in Zimbabwe for four years. I left Burundi when I was nine or ten. I want to share my story to inspire others who might hear my story, especially refugees.*

*

*My name is Alejandra. I'm twenty years old. I am from El Salvador. I've been living in Brisbane since I was two and I came here with my family. When I'm at uni, I study social sciences and arts. I deferred from uni this year to do a diploma in youth work, so that was really good. I work at a tutoring centre and I've been working there for like two years now. Why did I decide to share my story? I guess, I think it's a good story. I think that there is like perceptions of what refugees are like—just assumptions around that. I think not enough people have come into close contact with them.*

## "WELCOME" TO AUSTRALIA

When refugees arrive in Australia, they set foot in a complex context with its own unresolved colonial history, with its internal tensions and contradictions. They arrive in a nation-state that, historically, has had convoluted relationships with non-white inhabitants (Ang). Refugees arrive in a space that is neither neutral nor empty. They enter a space that is already contaminated "by racial power relations with a long colonial history, colonial imaginary, colonial knowledge and racial/ethnic hierarchies" (Grosfoguel et al. 641). Within the specific Australian settler-colonial history, a saga of dispossession and erasure of Indigenous peoples, paralleling deep fears of invasion from outsiders, provides an intensely complicated backdrop for new arrivals (Tascón 246).

This complicated settler-colonial backdrop was created in the late 1700s with land claims by the British, who, "under the legal fiction of Terra Nullius—land belonging to no-one—systematically dispossessed, murdered, raped and incarcerated the original owners" (Moreton-Robinson 24). The notion of nullius—"nothing, no one—no humans were here before the European arrived," is key. The colonial logic of white supremacy over the less-than-human Indigenous peoples is the basis of terra nullius and at the core of the logics that still govern the systems of power in charge of border control in Australia. And while the treatment of Indigenous peoples and non-white migrants (including refugees) has been different, with distinct historical trajectories, they both still occur and involve structural "practices of marginalisation and exclusion" (Rizvi 143).

In this dense narrative, the notion of terra nullius, even though discredited today, still takes centre stage. This very notion of land belonging to no one legitimizes the superiority-authority-ownership logics that entitle "dominant white Australia" and its institutions to determine who is allowed to enter the nation (Moreton-Robinson 25–26). This is a logic of colonial-patriarchal white sovereignty, with an elite group of settlers who see themselves as "local," in charge. Garbutt argues, "[W]e settler locals say we belong as though we and our culture have naturally emerged from the bounds of this place" (4). By occupying a hegemonic position in the nation-state, a "local" elite has had the ability to draw borders, geographical and symbolic, that demarcate spaces where certain groups of people can enter or not. It's within this intricate context—a space, place, time inhabited by voices from the in-between—that I write this letter.

## DEAR NAARIN, DANNY, ALEJANDRA, FAITH, MARY, GABRIELA, AND JESTOR,

Since Invasion Day,
the wind keeps blowing,
causing confusion.
Borders, barbed wire, walls
erected around the island nation.

White Australia policy is over.[5]
The island nation is now more diverse, multicultural…really?
But
the essence remains forcefully "white," "Western,"
with "Others" carefully kept on the margins.

And the man on TV says:
"The masses are coming,
displaced, uncontrollable.
Endless sea of faceless bodies
coming our way to spoil our stability,
our national identity.
Are they terrorists?
Are they a liability?"

People on the privileged side of the border are afraid.
Victims become the scapegoat
and governments invest
and thrive from this culture of panic.

Heated debate arises.

And the man on TV says:
"There is a solution,
Operation Sovereign Borders.[6]
We must protect 'our way of life!'
If you arrive by boat,
you will never resettle here,
indefinite mandatory detention,
even if you are a child."

"But where is our compassion?"
Someone from the privileged side of the border asks.

In response,
Australia says "welcome,"
to a carefully selected few,
including you.
About 15,000 lucky souls receive the "welcome" each year.[7]
Social services, support programs available to you.

You arrived, you are here.
But the wind keeps blowing,
causing confusion.
You have crossed Australia's physical border, but what does that mean?

You arrived in a new place, space, and time. You each come from different places, different trajectories. Each trajectory is unique, but in your new land, you will often be put into mental cages of homogenous experience, of solid categories, the "refugee," the "Other." It's windy over here, a land of confused identities.

I close my eyes. I think about the wind, crossing borders. I think about the stories you have told me. I can still hear your voices talking about your first experiences in Australia. And, as I write this letter, your voices appear again and again, fusing with my thoughts and conversations with Anzaldúa's voice/theories.

Your words are still fresh in my memory:
*Everything was different when we arrived here*
*I was only thirteen*
*My first impression was like "wow…what a clean green country"*
*Culture shock*
*We try to adapt*
*I really like it here but I don't feel very Aussie…*
*You get that: so where are* you *from?*
*I'm very happy we came, but I guess I just never felt like I could be fully embraced.*[8]

As I think about you and your families, I envision movements. You are still travelling; the travelling does not end as you arrive. The travelling will probably never end. A shift within yourself is happening. A shift is expected. You now inhabit a new place. Smiles.

> *You have to adapt...learn new things...see things in different ways but make sure that's not really changing you from positive to negative...Some [new] things can be conflicting [but being here] means that Australia is open for new people...And it's really a friendly nation...a place for opportunities...a place for brothers and sisters. (Faith)*

You keep smiling. You have been chosen within a complex entanglement of oppressions. Your suffering has been deemed valid and you managed to cross the border through the front gate. Fortunately, you didn't come by boat.

> *Asylum seekers who arrive by boat...are treated like animals, worse...if you come here like my family did, plane ticket, visa, there was a program for us... we had a home...I've read some stories about people [in detention centres] and it echoes my family's story but the only [difference] is that they didn't have access to apply for a visa. And that's something that could have so easily happened to us, so easily! (Alejandra)*

People on the privileged side of the border say "welcome," or do they? "Now learn the language, adapt to your new environment." This process is difficult for you, but it's much harder for your parents. All that is known has been broken. Family dynamics turned upside down. They, you, have to pick up the fragments of what's left and start anew.

> *When we arrived here it was like bang, the way people dressed, the language, the way people treated each other. It wasn't like aw I don't like these people... it was more like OK that's how they live and this is how we live and we were trying to adapt. [But] it's so much harder [for adults] because they have always lived in an environment, then they enter another that's completely different. My dad, I've seen him struggling...he tries to figure out things but then he forgets, which is really frustrating for him, that's kind of limiting his abilities. Sitting at home and doing nothing upsets him because he has always worked, all his life. (Naarin)*

Despite your efforts and struggles, the man on TV repeats like a chant: "Smile, be grateful, integrate—quickly." When I think about the man on TV and your stories of arrival, I start to wonder what's under the surface of welcoming smiles. What's hidden under the spotless, clean cities? The manicured backyards? What happens if you dig a little deeper? What might you find?

> *Sometimes you meet friendly people that will make you feel welcome. But sometimes...you meet people who are not so welcoming...Then you start questioning your identity to Australia and your purpose. (Mary)*

> *It can be kind of racist sometimes. I kind of have felt it before when I apply for a job...they look at your name and...probably won't call you back...My brother-in-law applied for jobs but they wouldn't call him...so he changed his name to John. (Danny)*

I understand you desire a place you can call "home." I'm not so sure what "home" means to you, but I believe you want to feel safe. You describe Australia as "a haven," a peaceful land. Yet, I keep wondering if you can or cannot cross the mighty walls of its symbolic borders.

> *Home for me is in Australia because I don't really have a home anymore in Burma because they don't want us. I have the feeling that here is home...I think that Australia accepts me as part of this place because [they gave us] residency. (Jestor)*

> *Here everything is OK, the way they treat me, I feel I'm like an Australian, the opportunities, the health, education, jobs, everything, I feel OK but I still feel I don't belong anywhere...not in Tanzania, not in Australia, not in Burundi...Sometimes it bothers me that I don't feel like I belong [anywhere]. (Gabriela)*

> *I don't really feel like I belong to this land, it's like 50/50...But at the same I'd like to live here because...it's safe and stable...[but] I always felt like I don't belong here cause I'm different, I look different. (Danny)*

When I hear your voice, your words, I feel that you are torn between the life you knew, the past represented by the faraway lands of your previous existence and the new demands of the place where you are supposed to construct your future. Perhaps part of your struggles is to create a sense of self. You want to be you. But what does that mean when you live in between potentially conflicting realities?

> *It is hard to play both the Muslim and the Australian girl. As you can tell, I'm not wearing the head scarf...I'd love to [wear it] but again there is a fear at the moment. Fear of how people would react to it and how I will be treated...There are times that you want to dress up certain way or go try out new things...yet, you don't give yourself permission as you will be breaking your religion rules, and you wouldn't want to disappoint your parents...we all want to break rules at times. (Naarin)*

Pain and confusion are central to your told experiences, yet not everything is bleak. You dream of a better future. You want to build your life anew in Australia. But where do you fit within a concept of "nation" that is still so contested? Claimed by an elite of white colonial settlers, desired by the displaced within the shiny lines of modernity, taken from the first Australians. Where do you fit within this contested landscape? Where do you fit within such a convoluted history of colonialism? You bring with you your complex history too; your body and soul are marked by the multiple layers of your travels, by gender, ethnicity, class, by your own displacements (Anzaldúa, *Borderlands*). Where do you fit? Where do you dwell?

I dare guess that you now inhabit a space in between. Not fully here or there, between here and over there, in the middle of nowhere.

## WELCOME TO THE AUSTRALIAN BORDERLANDS...[9]

> Borders are set up to define places that are safe and unsafe, to distinguish *us* from *them*. A border is a dividing line, a narrow strip along a steep edge. A borderland is a vague and undetermined place created by the emotional residue of an unnatural boundary. (Anzaldúa, *Borderlands* 25)

This ambiguous and vague space of constant transition, the direct consequence of artificial borders, is inhabited by people who challenge dominant rigid definitions of "normal." Never forget that notions of normalcy are heterogeneous, even within so-called mainstream cultures. Displacement, pain, discomfort, and creative forces co-inhabit the fertile grounds of the Borderlands. Here, a multitude of cultures meet and often clash. As Anzaldúa reminds us, here the fragmented pieces of complex identities can be pieced together or created anew (*Borderlands*). Transformation and healing spring from dwelling in this space. New perspectives emerge, and they are more than the sum of your broken pieces.

You are not quite an insider, but you are not completely out either. You push the boundaries of what it means to be Australian. You look different, sound different to the invented norms of Australianness. You inhabit an ambiguous position—at once settler and colonised. As Moreton-Robinson rightly points out, all non-Indigenous peoples who live in Australia are tied to migration, and all migration is linked to the dispossession of Indigenous Australians. That puts you (and me) in a complicated position. You are here escaping persecution in your homeland. You are the quintessential "*damné*" of the earth (Fanon), yet now you are a settler in Australia.

I believe you're well aware that this place in the cracks, between worlds, is difficult territory. Negotiation, mediation, bridge work are all part of the balance you and all people who live between realities endure on a daily basis (Anzaldúa, "(Un)Natural Bridges, (Un)Safe Spaces").

## CREATING NEW POSITIONALITIES FROM IN-BETWEEN

> While juggling several cultures or forces that clash, nepantleras live in tense balances entremedios, teetering on edges in states of entreguerras. (Anzaldúa, *Light in the Dark* 81)

> *When I was little, mum and dad wouldn't talk about here Australia, they would be talking about El Salvador...the culture at home was completely different to my friends at school...what was normal at school was not what was normal at home. (Alejandra)*

When I place your stories side by side, it strikes me how you speak of contrasts between the multiple worlds you inhabit. You speak about many messy encounters in your daily lives:

Linguistic clashes
Religious beliefs in contrast to Australian youth cultures
Changes of gender roles in the family
Being cast aside by accents and different looks

With your stories side by side, I see young people dwelling within, across, and between worlds: family, school, friends, broader society, religion.

I also realize that learning how to navigate these different and often-contradictory realities has been a central part of your journeys of being and becoming in the world(s). I see in you, seven young people drawing on your multiplicity in juggling acts where you constantly negotiate and attempt to cope. I'm then reminded that "living in intersections, in cusps, we must constantly operate in a negotiation mode" (Anzaldúa, *Light in the Dark* 71).

> *At around fourteen to sixteen, I felt like sometimes I just wanted to follow everyone and who cares what your country and your culture thinks. It wasn't very easy but I still managed my way around it. I feel better now. If it's a Western thing that I think it's good then I'll follow that but I still keep in mind my culture, if it's something bad then I rather keep my culture. (Mary)*

I also realize that as part of these juggling acts, you often function as linguistic and cultural bridges between your families and broader society.

> *The kids tend to learn the language faster than the parents,'til today we will help our lovely parents... we do help our family's friends as well. (Gabriela)*

In these processes, you cultivate vital coalitions with other Borderlands dwellers, building connections between your old and new realities.

> *It's easier to make friends with people from a similar background because we have something in common; it's easier to connect to people from a refugee background. We get each other. (Danny)*

> *Because you've all been in that 'boat' of adapting, understanding the new cultures, even though we are from all over the place. It's so much easier to communicate and be friends; we don't have to explain everything we do or believe in. (Naarin)*

From your stories, side by side, I also see an imagined over-there that becomes reality through your parents' stories and memories. This reality is different from the space where you now dwell, Australia, giving "rise to an elsewhere-within-here" (Trinh 37). And as I reflect on your experiences of juggling an "elsewhere-within-here" and contrasting worlds within daily lives, I keep thinking of windy days, where objects are blown about, where dust sometimes blocks visions, with people moving around frantically, trying to make sense of the mess. I envision you walking through the wind, your words swirling in the air and landing on these pages. From these moving words, as you juggle complex experiences in windy days, you create coping strategies. I believe that from these rather complicated situations, you create new positionalities from in-between.

In my imagination, you continue walking through the wind, you clear away the dust from your eyes, and as Lugones would say, you negotiate multiple worlds every day as part of your existence (18). You are not comfortable, but you are determined to deal with challenges. From this negotiation mode, from complex positionalities between worlds, unique perspectives and the possibility of fluency in the many worlds you have contact with are possible (*Light in the Dark*). I glimpse eyes being cleared; I also start clearing mine. I see that each Borderlands dweller has particular ways of dealing with daily life. So, dwelling in this space is not an essentialized experience with fixed definitions and demarcations. Yet there are commonalities from your told experiences I wish to stress:

Fluid identities emerge
Fluid, hybrid categories are possible
Mixed
You are neither of your identity markers
You are all of them
You are more than the added fragments of the multiple you

In this windy space of contradictions and connections, people develop a deep tolerance for ambiguity, and that is key to your survival (Anzaldúa, *Borderlands*). And as you navigate the Borderlands, you "undergo the anguish of changing...perspectives and crossing a series of cruz calles, junctures, and thresholds, some leading to a different way of relating to people and surroundings and others to the creation of a new world" (Anzaldúa, *Light in the Dark* 17).

## WINDY DAYS

I really do not like windy days. They make me feel uncomfortable and nervous. But I cannot control the wind, so I have to learn how to live with it. Writing this letter to you has felt like strong gusts of wind were about to blow me away. As I type, I see a bit of me in your struggles to belong, to find home, as I also attempt to find a space where I can dwell, be, know, and speak in this ambiguous place called Australia. I see similarities, but I see differences. I think of the impossibility, indeed, the futility, of homogenizing migrant and refugee experiences. I see worlds "replete with contradictions, riddled with cracks" (Anzaldúa, *Light in the Dark* 74).

Here, in this windy place, definitions of and boundaries around concepts of home and belonging are also fluid and part of constant negotiation modes. Likewise, movement is not necessarily related to the physical and concrete.

> *The greatest movements occur within the self...for even individuals who have not left the nation, region or town in which they were born, have not necessarily stayed at home, and if they have stayed at home, it is not necessarily the case that they have not moved. (Ahmed et al. 7)*

I believe that in these movements and negotiations within the self, new fragile "homes" are built in spaces between, in the Australian Borderlands.

I also start to realize that my mind is much more colonised than I have ever expected. Rigid categories and essentialisms are pertinent legacies of coloniality within my being. I now begin to have a glimpse of nuances and complexities as you slowly free yourself from my mental cages. In this process, you challenge strict, fragmented categories, "the refugee," the "victim," the "Other," the "traumatized" one.

As I bring this letter to an end and come to fluid, ever-evolving, partial conclusions, I hear Anzaldúa's voice once again, like a soft breeze, guiding us, irradiating our paths:

> *[We] construct alternative roads, creating new topographies and geographies of hybrid selves who transcend binaries… Navigating the cracks is the process of reconstructing life anew, of fashioning new identities. [We] use competing systems of knowledge and rewrite [our] identities.… Like tender green shoots growing out of the cracks, [we] eventually overturn foundations, making conventional definitions of otherness hard to sustain. (Light in the Dark 82–84)*

Yours,
Fabiane

## NOTES

1. My participation at the 2016 SSGA El Mundo Zurdo Conference and, consequently, the creation of this piece was made possible by the University of Queensland Graduate School International Travel Grant, of which I was a recipient in 2016. I also would like to express my infinite gratitude to the seven people who generously shared their stories with me and to my supervisors, Liz Mackinlay and Bob Lingard, for their immense support.

2. As I engage Anzaldúa's concepts, I continue employing the term "Borderlands." I acknowledge and respect her shift to 'nepantla,' but I choose to use "Borderlands" to refer to "in-between spaces" because of its stronger semantic impact for Australian audiences. And on the note of context, I understand that Australia is clearly far from and different from the US/Mexico border. Both places have in common links between locations of exclusion, marginality, Borderlands (as physical and socially constructed spaces), and processes of colonisation/creation of "nation" sates. Yet their histories of colonisation/entanglement of oppressions/structures of power are distinct, and I recognize the dangers of simplifying complex differences. So, when I write about the Australian Borderlands, I do not ignore the concept's particularities, and I take into consideration the socio-political, historical, and geographical differences between the Australian national context and the Mexico/US border where Anzaldúa developed her theories.

3. The told experiences at the centre of this piece come from a series of interviews that took place in Brisbane, Australia in 2015, with seven people who shared their stories of migration to Australia. For confidentiality reasons, pseudonyms were used. They were chosen by research partners.

4. I use italics to represent research partners' words from interview transcripts.

5. The Migration Restriction Act of 1901, which became known as the White Australia Policy, was created in 1901 and remained in place until 1966. It aimed to restrict numbers of non-white migrants to Australia ("White Australia Policy"). This policy—together with numerous "Aborigines' Acts"—was fundamental to formalising national "racist beliefs and practices" and reinforce "the erasure and exclusion of 'coloured' peoples" as part of its foundational history as a nation (Tascón 245).

6. Operation Sovereign Borders is an Australian military-led border control initiative put into place in 2013 by the newly elected conservative government (Asylum Seeker Resource Centre). With the objective of "turning back the boats" and "deterring people-smugglers," any asylum seeker who arrives by boat while this policy is in place is excluded from the possibility of resettling in Australia. A consequence of this policy has been a decrease in number of boat arrivals at the cost of numerous asylum seekers who are left indefinitely in transit countries or in offshore detention centres (Asylum Seeker Resource Centre).

7. In Australia in the period 2015-16, the Refugee and Humanitarian Program granted a total of 17,555 visas (Australian Human Rights Commission). Within this total, 15,552 visas were given to resettlement applicants (people who apply for visas whilst in transit countries) and 2,003 visas under the onshore protection component (Australian Human Rights Commission). Refugees who arrive under the Humanitarian Program in Australia receive a range of services by the government and community organizations to assist them with the resettlement process (Puvimanasinghe et al. 314). Everyone who shared their stories for this project arrived in Australia as part of the Humanitarian Program.

8. Mixed statements from interviews in which people talked about their first impressions of Australia.

9. This discussion about Borderlands is based on Anzaldúa's writings in "(Un)Natural Bridges, (Un)Safe Spaces"; *Borderlands/La Frontera: The New Mestiza*; *Making Face, Making Soul/ Haciendo Caras* (especially "En rapport, In Opposition: Cobrando cuentas a la nuestra"); and *Light in the Dark/Luz en lo oscuro*.

## WORKS CITED

Ahmed, Sara, et al. "Introduction: Uprootings/Regroundings: Questions of Home and Migration." *Uprootings/Regroundings: Questions of Home and Migration*, edited by Sara Ahmed et al., Berg, 2003, pp. 1–19.

Ang, Ien. *On Not Speaking Chinese: Living Between Asia and the West.* Routledge, 2001.

Anzaldúa, Gloria. *Borderlands/La Frontera: The New Mestiza.* 1987. 4th ed., Aunt Lute, 2012.

---. "En rapport, In Opposition: Cobrando cuentas a la nuestra." *Making Face, Making Soul/ Haciendo Caras*, edited by Gloria Anzaldúa, Aunt Lute, 1990, pp. 142–150.

---. *Light in the Dark/Luz en lo oscuro.* Duke UP, 2015.

---. "On the Process of Writing *Borderlands/La Frontera.*" *The Gloria Anzaldúa Reader*, edited by AnaLouise Keating, Duke UP, 2009, pp. 187–197.

---. "(Un)Natural Bridges, (Un)Safe Spaces." *this bridge we call home: radical visions for transformation*, edited by Gloria Anzaldúa and Ana Louise Keating, Routledge, 2002, pp. 1–5.

Asylum Seeker Resource Centre. "Operation Sovereign Borders." 2013, www.asrc.org.au/wp-content/uploads/2013/07/Operation-Sovereign-Borders-May-2014.pdf. Accessed 1 Oct. 2016.

Australian Human Rights Commission. *Asylum Seekers, Refugees and Human Rights Snapshot Report.* 2nd ed., Australian Human Rights Commission, 2017.

Fanon, Frantz. *The Wretched of the Earth.* Grove Press, 1961.

Garbutt, Robert. *The Locals: Identity, Place and Belonging in Australia and Beyond.* Peter Lang, 2011.

Grosfoguel, Ramon, et al. "'Racism,' Intersectionality and Migration Studies: Framing Some Theoretical Reflections." *Identities: Global Studies in Culture and Power*, vol. 22, no. 6, 2015, pp. 635–652.

Lugones, Maria. *Pilgrimages/Peregrinajes: Theorizing Coalition against Multiple Oppressions.* Rowman & Littlefield, 2003.

Moreton-Robinson, Aileen. "'I Still Call Australia Home: Belonging, Place, Indigeneity and Whiteness in a Postcolonising Society." *Uprootings/Regroundings: Questions of Home and Migration*, edited by Sara Ahmed et al., Berg, 2003, pp. 23–40.

"White Australia Policy." *National Museum of Australia.* www.nma.gov.au/online_features/defining_ moments/featured/white_australia_policy _begins. Accessed 1 Oct. 2016.

Puvimanasinghe, Teresa, et al. ""Giving Back to Society What Society Gave Us": Altruism, Coping, and Meaning Making by Two Refugee Communities in South Australia." *Australian Psychologist*, vol. 49, no. 5, 2014, pp. 313–321.

Rizvi, Fasil. *Colonialism and Postcolonial Theory.* Sage, 2014.

Tascón, Sonia Magdalena. "Refugees and the Coloniality of Power: Border-Crossers of Postcolonial Whiteness." *Whitening Race: Essays in Social and Cultural Criticism*, edited by Aileen Moreton-Robinson, Aboriginal Studies, 2004, pp. 239–253.

Trinh, Min-ha T. *Elsewhere, Within Here: Immigration, Refugeeism and the Boundary Event.* Taylor and Francis, 2011.

# IMMIGRATION, SURVEILLANCE, AND UNACCOMPANIED MINORS IN THE RIO GRANDE VALLEY

## NEPANTLA PRAXIS IN THE WORKS OF BORDERLAND ARTIST CELESTE DE LUNA

VERONICA SANDOVAL, LADY MARIPOSA

Gloria Anzaldúa asserts, "Border arte is an art that supersedes the pictorial. It depicts both the soul del artista y el alma del pueblo [the soul of the artist and the soul of the Pueblo]. It deals with who tells the stories and what stories and histories are told" ("Border Arte" 62). Anzaldúa calls this form of visual narrative "autohistoria," a form that "goes beyond the traditional self-portrait or autobiography...[to tell the artist's] personal story...[and] include[s their] cultural history" (62). By analyzing the work of nepantleros and nepantleras currently living, working, and creating in the borderlands, I will highlight Anzaldúa's theory in praxis, where artists live in "the locus of resistance, of rupture, of implosion and explosion," where, through their work, borderland artists "[put] together fragments and [create new assemblages]" of the realities they live in (49). At the center of this essay is borderland nepantlera Celeste De Luna, whose haunting images of anchor babies, detention centers, checkpoints, and Aztec deities speak directly to Anzaldúa's nepantla theory as a threshold of transformation. The border as a "historical and metaphorical site" is an occupied site where border artists strive to decolonize space through their art (63), and, thus, De Luna's work is a prime example of the ways in which nepantleras decolonize narratives, stirring political consciousness. Through her recognition of the systems at play that change the trajectory of her work and her family's life, De

Luna's work is an autohistoria that demonstrates a refusal to remain silent about a shifting social and political landscape that implicates all of those living in and trapped within the borderlands.

## POLICING EXPRESSWAYS, THE INVISIBLE WALL

The changes in the Rio Grande Valley of Texas within the last five years are not subtle. In the summer of 2016, during my extended return home, I witnessed a significant addition to the borderlands: an increase in police surveillance. During my routine commutes into McAllen, I encountered six state troopers and two border patrol agents on average within the first eight miles of my trip between La Joya and Sullivan City. The small town of Sullivan, where I grew up and where my parents have lived for the last twenty-one years, is among one of the many borderland communities that are aided in the "security" of community members by the agencies that patrol Expressway 83. In their *2020 Vision and Strategy*, the US Customs and Immigration Department call this "integrated operation planning and execution, a crucial element to detecting, interdicting, and disrupting illegal cross-border activities" (22). This alliance between federal and local law enforcement is meant "to develop a seamless network of integrated law enforcement capabilities that [span] the border environment" (22). The framework for this type of integrated operation was laid out in 2001 through the USA PATRIOT Act, which "facilitated information sharing and cooperation among government agencies so that they [could] better 'connect the dots'" (United States Department of Justice). For those who have lived and currently live in the borderlands of South Texas, this network is indeed seamless, especially in Sullivan City, a town located within three miles of the Rio Bravo. In this border-plex, all law enforcement agencies meld into a contiguous machine, watching us, questioning us, protecting us for our own good—while big rigs power by in a hiss of air, transporting commerce in discreet metal containers at all hours of the day and night, leaving diesel melting into roads that lead north and south.

In "now let us shift," Anzaldúa writes,

> humanity [is] undergoing profound transformations and shifts in perception.…We are experiencing a personal, global identity crisis in a disintegrating social order that possesses little heart and functions to oppress people by organizing them into hierarchies of commerce and power—a collusion of government, transnational industry, business, and the military, all linked by a pragmatic technology and science voracious for money and control. (118)

Perhaps no other image captures the exploitation of criminalized brown bodies in the borderlands more appropriately than Celeste De Luna's *East: El Corralón*. De Luna elaborated on *El Corralón* during "A Platica with Celeste De Luna," an online interview with Iris Rodriguez for *Xicana Chronicles* published in September of 2014. In this plática, she discusses the post-9/11 political atmosphere and the ways in which members of the media were thick with fear and frenzy over immigrant brown bodies and brown people. She describes immigration and borders in the Rio Grande Valley pre-9/11 as porous, with residents maintaining their connections to both sides of the border through social and family ties. Of particular interest to De Luna is the Raymondville Detention Center, known as "Tent City," which she calls "visibly stimulating" with its oval-shaped tents, chain-link fence, and barbed wire sparkling in the sun ("Platica"). It was unsettling to her that no one would talk about Tent City, or how overlooking Tent City was the eerie sight of the Raymondville water tower, which De Luna said looked as if the Giant "R" was a smiling emoticon. "How horrible…to be in this place…and …look up at this smiling face" ("Platica").

**Fig. 1. *East: El Corralón.* Artist Celeste De Luna. 2012. Acrylic on canvas. Artist's private collection. La Feria, Texas.**

At first glance, *El Corralón* appears to depict Tent City prisoners who wear orange jumpsuits and extend their open arms toward money raining from the Raymondville water tower; however, a close examination reveals that what look like hands towards the sky are actually monarch butterfly wings. Within the background of *El Corralón*, a detention yard contains facility tents and detainees with monarch wings, who stand in rows among detainees without wings. Yet it is an officer who is central subject of *El Corralón.* He stands guard before the detention yard. From his back a skeletal set of capillary wings seems to both melt and become entangled with the chain link fence that disappears behind him. These wings mark subjects in *El Corralón* as related, and as such, these symbols become a commentary on the people of color who work the various local and state apparatuses that patrol the borderlands. Their work for these apparatuses inevitably means the deportation and criminalization of undocumented immigrants entering the US from the country of their ancestry, and this reality is not lost on De Luna. The ambiguity of the officer's wings lends itself to multiple interpretations. The skeletal framework suggests the wings were once, like those of the detainees behind him, monarch wings which lost their membrane to the devouring fence. Alternately, his wings are doing what butterfly wings are meant to do: camouflaging the officer for his protection within the correctional institution that employs him. Perhaps his skeletal framework, with its tinted red hue along the ridges of the tubular veins, connotes the surging of blood, a mending of a torn relationship, as the officer struggles to heal back the monarch membrane that marks him as those he detains.

For the central subject of *El Corralón*, the lines between culpability and complacency, alliances and rebellion, vendido and sobrevivendo, become blurred in every detail of De Luna's work. The star on the officer's chest is a badge over a Star of David, a vivid reminder of the past, asking the viewer to make larger connections to historical atrocities that have targeted other persecuted groups. Detentions like these have happened before, tent cities like Raymondville's detention center are a throwback to the Japanese incarceration camps that were run in Texas during the 1940s. For the people of color who continue to be recruited into well-paid governmental positions like US Customs and Border Protection as well as Immigration and Customs Enforcement, the Star of David in *El Corralón* critically marks them as both oppressor and oppressed; an identifier for the complications of maneuvering their own people's history in the new history being written with their brown bodies as tools through the continued militarization of the US-Mexico border.

In her online plática, De Luna goes on to discuss space and the ways in which the Rio Grande Valley seems disconnected from the rest of Texas. Between the checkpoints and the implementation of the border wall after 9/11, De Luna described the borderlands as literally "fenced in" ("Platica"). As expressed by Anzaldúa, "the Mexican immigrant at the moment of crossing the barbed-wired fence into a hostile 'paradise' of El Norte (the U.S.) is caught in a state of nepantla" ("Border Arte" 56). Because of the virtual fence of surveillance sectioning off the borderlands of the Rio Grande Valley from the rest of Texas, and, subsequently, the United States, many of the trapped inhabitants of this region have become nepantleros/nepantleras. Throughout many of the gatherings I attended while socializing with friends during the summer of 2016, the repeated theme of "being fenced in" found its way into conversations on political climate and discourse on subject matter in the art being created in the Rio Grande Valley. A close friend explained how the number of undocumented immigrants had risen, and that those people, trapped between el Rio Bravo and the Texas checkpoints, were changing the political rhetoric at the various poetry readings across the Valley. Poetry readings in Brownsville were now filled with poets who write in Spanish and whose shows were attended by large numbers of Spanish-speaking community members. The work and events of these new nepantleros/nepantleras were described as powerful and political, work that spoke directly to the realities of the borderlands.[1] De Luna states that her motivation for the theme of her 2013 *El Corralón* was the need to address the changes that were happening through the separation of the Rio Grande Valley via detention centers, checkpoints, and the border wall—changes which she understood as having physical, spiritual, psychological, and environmental effects on the region ("Platica"). True to her observation, these changes and the perceived separation between the Valley and the rest of the state are found in the narratives emphasized by present-day nepantleros/nepantleras.

## ART FROM THE FOUR CORNERS: THE PROFIT OF UNACCOMPANIED MINORS

*El Corralón*, as part of De Luna's larger narrative about the borderlands, captures the complications of living within the Rio Grande Valley. For De Luna, however, it is necessary to extend her critique to the four corners of el Valle, and she bridges the complexities of this geopolitical space through an interactive art experience. Anzaldúa describes nepantla as a "threshold of transformation.... the place where at once we are detached (separated) and attached (connected) to each of our several cultures. Here the watcher on the bridge (nepantla) can 'see through' the larger symbolic process that's trying to become conscious through a particular life situation or event" ("Border Arte" 56). In her installation *Nepantla: Art from the Four Corners of the Valley—El Corralón, Las Garritas, Muros, y Puentes*, De Luna recreates a bridge; as a nepantlera, she helps those interacting with her installation to make a spiritual and psychic crossing, guiding them through the processes of transformation, a process Anzaldúa called conocimiento ("Let us be" 17). During the months of August through October 2014 at South Texas College, De Luna displayed an installation that included four pieces on opposing walls. She created a spot in the center of the room to stand, where the viewer could be the literal watcher on the bridge. The pieces displayed in *Nepantla* include North, South, East, and West components, *East:*

**Fig. 2. *Nepantla: Art from the Four Corners of the Valley* exhibit. Installation. 2013. South Texas College Hispanic Heritage Month. McAllen, Texas.**

*El Corralón*, *North: Las Garritas*, *West: El Muro*, and *South: Point of Entry*. In this formation, *Nepantla* captures the Rio Grande Valley, a spot on earth that contains all other places within it, crossing all dimension of sky, spirit, space, and earth (Anzaldúa, "Border Arte" 57).

**Fig. 3. *North: Las Garritas*. Artist Celeste De Luna. 2012. Acrylic and mixed media on canvas. Artist's private collection. La Ferria, Texas.**

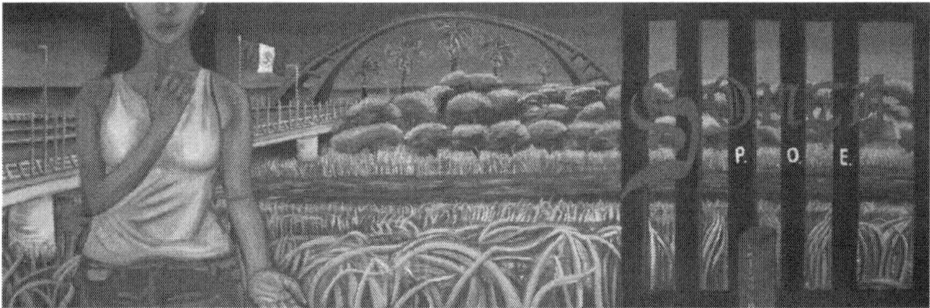


**Fig. 4. *South: Point of Entry*. Artist Celeste De Luna. 2012. Acrylic on canvas. Artist's private collection. La Ferria, Texas.**

**Fig. 5. *West: El Muro*. Artist Celeste De Luna. 2012. Acrylic on canvas. Artist's private collection. La Ferria, Texas.**

In this installation, De Luna draped her East section with an orange fence-like mesh, and on this mesh, she pinned monarch butterflies as if trapped between worlds. The migration of monarch butterflies has become a metaphor in many Chicanx art pieces and is featured often in various immigration campaigns. Not ironically, McAllen, the town where the exhibit was located, would soon see an influx of unaccompanied minors, which would escalate in 2014. The town bore

**Fig. 6. Detail. *Nepantla: Art from the Four Corners of the Valley* exhibit. Installation. 2013. South Texas College Hispanic Heritage Month. McAllen, Texas.**

witness to a flutter of new migration of predominately Central American children fleeing poverty and killings in their home countries. The children who sought entry into the US in 2014 were not born here, therefore not "anchoring" their mother's citizenship. Instead they ensured their own survival via migration to the United States, anchoring hope to the countless families the minors left behind. In May 2014, *The Monitor* newspaper reported that, for Homeland Security Secretary Jeh Johnson, "young immigrants became a more 'vivid' issue after he spent Mother's Day with his wife in McAllen, where he met a 12-year-old girl and asked where her mother was. The girl tearfully told the Homeland Security chief that she has no mother and that she was hoping to find her father, who lives somewhere in the U.S." ("Witnessing surge"). Johnson's concern prompted him "to declare a 'level-four condition of readiness' in the Rio Grande Valley." However, his observation expressed no real concern to address the underlying issues that cause mass migrations. Instead, Johnson stated, "We have to discourage parents from sending or sending for their children to cross the Southwest border because of the risks involved.…A South Texas processing center is no place for a child" ("Witnessing surge"). Johnson's short-sighted comments feign concern for undocumented children due to "the risks involved"; however, Johnson does not consider "the risks" that children face in their home countries, risks that parents deem urgent enough to become separated from their children. He also does not consider what it means to tell members of families that they need to ignore their desire to be reunited with their children. Such feigned concern, draped in the language of "need" and "well-being" of children, becomes a platform for the deployment of federal dollars. In his February 18, 2015 State Address, Texas Governor Greg Abbott again employed "welfare of children" in his political rhetoric, this time concerning himself with the safety of "Latino" children.

> On one of my many visits to the Rio Grande Valley, I met a young Latina who pleaded with me to keep my promise to secure the border. She told me about her younger brother being in a pick-up soccer game where kids were choosing up teams. But one of the boys was a child of a known cartel member.
>
> Should her brother pick the boy for his team? What would be the consequences be if he did? If he didn't? Our children should not be faced with such tough choices. We will not fail that young Latina. We will not fail my fellow Texans. We will do what the federal government has failed to do. We will secure our border. (Taylor)

Abbott, with "anguish" over the tough decisions that children may have to make over the selection of team members in a soccer game, then goes on to mandate the legislature to fast track solutions on the issue of immigration. Banking on the culture of crisis and anti-immigrant rhetoric, Abbott's fast-tracked solution is his own proposal for spending $735 million in Fiscal Year 2016–2017 on border security (Taylor). His spending bill, which was passed in May 2015, contains millions of dollars to be spent on increasing the already-heavily surveilled and patrolled Southwest Border. The bill introduces "$91.8 million to allow DPS to hire and deploy at least 250 new Texas state troopers during 2016–17, with a goal of adding another 250 during 2018–19. That's 500 new troopers over four years…The Governor's Budget [also] includes $10 million to provide local law enforcement agencies with the tools to increase their effectiveness with more staff and resources" (Taylor). The dangers involved with entering the US without documentation already disproportionately affect women and children; however, with this massive influx of money into state policing, the potential danger of migration through the Rio Grande Valley is extended from the initial crossing of the Rio Bravo and the South Texas checkpoints, to, now, the entire state of Texas. Centering women and children subjects' bodies—bodies devoured by the machine of neo-colonialism, trapped behind chain-link fences and barbed wire—in her compositions, De Luna's work continues to highlight this grim reality.

### *BORDER HEADS & AMERICA THE BEAUTIFUL*

Although Johnson can claim that a processing center is no place for children, for-profit detention centers and their increase in revenue would suggest otherwise. Corrections Corporation of America, the largest owner of partnership correctional, detention, and reentry facilities in America, released its financial results for the first quarter of 2016, showing a revenue of $447.4 million, which is an increase of 5.0% from the prior year's quarter (Hopewell). They state, "Financial performance was driven primarily by stronger than anticipated demand from our federal partners, most notably Immigration and Customs Enforcement" (Hopewell).

**Fig. 7. *Border Heads*. Artist Celeste De Luna. 2014. Lithograph. Artist's private collection. La Ferria, Texas.**

Corrections Corporation of America's investment in the detention of undocumented immigrants and the United States' stringent immigration policies and geopolitical strategies consequently ensure the continued migration, and, unfortunately, the continued death of men, women, and children. De Luna's *Border Heads* and *America the Beautiful* are powerful commentaries about the US's continued investment in detention centers, particularly in the detention of children. De Luna's ability to create potent political commentary lies in not just the morbidity of the images, but also in what Anzaldúa observed as she walked in the open market exhibit in the Denver Museum of Natural History. Anzaldúa thought "of how border art, in critiquing old, traditional, and erroneous representations of the Mexico-U.S. border, attempts to represent the 'real world' de la gente going about their daily lives… [But in looking beyond] the tangible, one sees a connection to the spirit world, to the underworld, and to other realities" ("Border Arte" 54). De Luna etches those tangible realities of detention centers, walls, and bridges into connections with the spirit world and with "other realties"—realties that are overlooked as detained children become pawns for the state and perching posts for politicians to crow about surveillance, mass deportation, and militarization.

These pieces, which De Luna calls "homage[s] to the migrant children border crisis of 2014" and "tribute[s] to all the Mexican and Central American children who…died crossing the border to seek a better life," were displayed during the South Texas College Human Rights Show in 2015 (*Border Heads*). De Luna said of *Border Heads* that it occurred to her, "[S]ome American attitudes towards the children of the crisis were particularly cruel and medieval. Perhaps, if cruelty ruled the day, some people would see these children's heads on spikes atop of the border wall" ( "STC Human Rights"). In *America the Beautiful*, "images of the border wall and the razor wire of detention camps, which are ever present in the immigration experience, [are depicted, along with] the Mexican death/earth goddess Coatlicue, who throws her hands up in the air and rolls her eyes at a new offering, a migrant child pawn. On the pedestal itself are the words 'America the Beautiful'" ("STC Human Rights"). The integration of Coatlicue into the political commentary of immigration policies depicts the climate of the Rio

**Fig. 8. *America the Beautiful.* Artist Celeste De Luna. 2014. Lithograph. Artist's private collection. La Ferria, Texas.**

Grande Valley in its own Coatlicue state, "an intensely negative channel...caged in a private hell; [where residents] feel angry, fearful, hopeless, and depressed" (Anzaldúa, "now let us shift" 150). De Luna's work is a prime example of nepantla art, life captured in the borderlands, which "renders that world and its people in more than mere surface slices" (Anzaldúa, "Border Arte" 54). Anzaldúa explains that those in the Coatlicue state feel peace, happiness, and love in spaces which are cultivated by nepantleros/nepantleras ("now let us shift" 150–151) For artists like De Luna and others creating political discourse in their work, nepantleros/nepantleras seek to release la Coatlicue, becoming those who take matters into their own hands, and eventually taking dominion over serpents (*Borderlands* 73).

## SLEEPING WITH THE ENEMY: AUTOHISTORIA AND MAKING SOUL

De Luna's work is a living, breathing center that reflects her life, her work excavating the art that her world already contains, with each piece unearthing a story that feels, looks, and sounds like life in the borderlands. In "Flights of the Imagination: Rereading/Rewriting Realties," Anzaldúa refers to that which some call "love" that "stirs artist to take action, [propelling them] toward the act of making," and names it "conocimiento." "This conocimiento initiates the relationship between self-knowledge and creative work, [and] because the artist must keep watch [of] her inner responses, she becomes more aware, more alive, and thus she 'makes' the story of herself as she makes her art" (40). De Luna's political artistry is critical of not only the systems that impact geopolitical borders but also her own positionality.

In a June 2015 blog entitled "Sleeping with the Enemy, Part I," De Luna responded to an *Oxford American Magazine* article that had been released earlier that spring. In the article, "Art Against the Wall," author Stephanie Elizondo Griest asks her white male tour guide, a non-native of the Rio Grande Valley and a Brownsville gallery owner, about Texas artists who infuse politics into their work. After the gallery owner listed only male political artists, Griest asked why he only mentioned men; he replied that "he knew [of] a talented Chicana artist with a taste for subversive work, but she couldn't quench it because her husband works for U.S. Immigration and Customs Enforcement. 'You can't bite the hand that feeds you,' he said" (Elizondo Griest). De Luna's impassioned response was released in a blog entry entitled "Sleeping with the Enemy," a post that directly calls out the racist and sexist remarks that accused De Luna of being apolitical due to her relationship with the man she married. In response to the assertion that there are no women in the Rio Grande Valley engaging in political art, De Luna notes, "If you can't find women border artists, it's because you're not looking hard enough" ("Sleeping with the Enemy"). De Luna goes on to explain, "The idea that people of the RGV are apolitical people fosters the dangerous myth that the plight of this region (drugs, poverty, and violence) is really due to apathy, laziness, and criminality and not violent, racist government structures, both American and Mexican. There is a Spanish saying that you hear the real radicals throw around, "Sin Mujer, no hay revolución" ("Sleeping with the Enemy"). Since then, Elizondo Griest has reached out to De Luna to correct the record, with Elizondo Griest interviewing De Luna for her new 2017 book entitled *All the Agents and Saints: Dispatches from the U.S. Borderlands.*

De Luna's "Sleeping with the Enemy Part II" also discusses the relationship with her husband whom she calls "Juan." Pre-9/11, Juan was attempting to work through his citizenship paperwork and apply for a job in a federal facility. With his military background and refusing to apply as a border patrol agent, Juan instead sought a job with Immigration and Naturalization Services (INS). Post 9/11, the INS would eventually be merged into ICE, and her husband would end up employed in the very same capacity he had been trying to avoid. De Luna lays out a timeline of how her husband, who, for several years, refused to give up his Salvadoran citizenship, became an ICE agent in 2003. She identifies as well the start of her political Chicana consciousness in 2002: "Although Juan's work has caused much tension and even trauma in our lives, we have kept our family together. As an artist who creates political artwork that directly disagrees with I.C.E. policies, I am my own person who has strong opinions and beliefs. My artwork reflects my personal experiences and my voice is not hindered by anyone, anything, or any government agency" ("Sleeping with the Enemy II").

## CONCLUSION: RECONCILING CONFLICTING IMPULSES

De Luna recognizes the systems in play that changed the trajectory of her family's life, but does not remain silent about her shifting positionality. Instead, through her visual narratives, she incorporates her own autohistoria into pieces like *El Corralón*. Several years ago, when I first saw *El Corralón*, and before I knew De Luna and her work well enough to know of her husband's profession, I envisioned this piece as generalized political commentary from an artist who grew up in the Rio Grande Valley. I imagined the central subject as a reflection of the many individuals who work in detention centers or as border patrol agents, never thinking that the reference that De Luna was making was much more personal. Unless you are familiar with De Luna's family life, you will not have known that *El Corralón* directly references her husband Juan. Anzaldúa calls creativity a liberatory impulse, a process that "demands the reconciliation of conflicting impulses and ideas" ("Flight of the Imagination" 40). De Luna, through the inclusion of her husband as a central subject, reconciles the conflicting impulses and ideas of her family life. The man with ossified capillary wings guarding the prisoners in *El Corralón is* her husband Juan, even inscribing on the guard "El Sal," for El Salvador, as a way to mark the man as Juan.

De Luna's work is political and unapologetically subversive, her continued critical commentary on borderland politics and policies goes beyond telling her personal story, and includes the cultural history that shapes the Rio Grande Valley ("Border Arte" 62). As De Luna states in an interview with Stephanie Elizondo Griest, "Migrants aren't the only ones trapped in nepantla, the state of in-between-ness that transpires from straddling worlds. Such is the fate of every member of the borderland, no matter what documents we carry." Griest concurs, "Everybody is caught up in the system together" (*All the Agents and Saints* 80–81). The border as a "historical and metaphorical site" is an occupied site where border artists strive to decolonize space through their art ("Border Arte" 63), and De Luna's work continues to propel her towards action, decolonizing narratives, and stirring political consciousness. Her act of making art through conocimiento, what I choose to call an act of love, a stirring to creation (Anzaldúa, "Flights of the Imagination" 41), is what Xicanas like me, who live in the Pacific Northwest and ache for our borderland home, devour to not forget, devour to remember.

## NOTES

1. Chisme from my close personal friend, 2015–2017 McAllen Poet Laureate Priscilla Celina Suarez, during breakfast in discussing her appearance and performance schedule across the Rio Grande Valley since becoming Poet Laureate. https://www.facebook.com/priscilla.suarez

## WORKS CITED

Anzaldúa, Gloria. "Border Arte: Nepantla, el lugar de la frontera." *Light in the Dark/Luz en lo Oscuro: Rewriting Identity, Spirituality, Reality*, edited by AnaLouise Keating, Duke UP, 2015, pp. 47–64.

---. *Borderlands/La Frontera: The New Mestiza*. 1987. 3rd ed., Aunt Lute, 2007.

---. "Flights of the Imagination: Rereading/Rewriting Realities." *Light in the Dark/Luz en lo Oscuro: Rewriting Identity, Spirituality, Reality*, edited by AnaLouise Keating, Duke UP, 2015, pp. 23–46.

---. "Let us be the healing of the wound: The Coyolxauhqui imperative—La sombra y el sueño." *Light in the Dark/Luz en lo Oscuro: Rewriting Identity, Spirituality, Reality*, edited by AnaLouise Keating, Duke UP, 2015, pp. 9–22.

---. "now let us shift...conocimiento...inner work, public acts." *Light in the Dark/Luz en lo Oscuro: Rewriting Identity, Spirituality, Reality*, edited by AnaLouise Keating, Duke UP, 2015, pp. 117–159.

De Luna, Celeste. *America the Beautiful*. 2014, lithograph, artist's private collection, La Ferria, Texas.

---. *Border Heads*. 2014, lithograph, artist's private collection, La Ferria, Texas.

---. "Border Heads Artist Statement." *Academia.edu*, November 2015, www.academia.edu/11515856/Border_Heads. Accessed 1 Sept. 2016.

---. *East: El Corralón*. 2012, acrylic on canvas, artist's private collection, La Ferria, Texas.

---. "STC Human Rights Artist Statement." *Academia.edu*, November 2015, www.academia.edu/11529578/2015_STC_Human_Rights_Show_Artist_Statement. Accessed 1 Sept. 2016.

---. *Nepantla: Art from the Four Corners of the Valley*. Aug.-Oct. 2013, exhibit/installation, STC Hispanic Heritage Month, South Texas College, McAllen, Texas.

---. *North: Las Garritas*. 2012, acrylic and mixed media on canvas, artist's private collection, La Ferria, Texas.

---. "A Platica with Celeste De Luna: Artist and Print Maker." Interview by Iris Rodriguez. *Xicanachronicles.com*, 5 Sept. 2015, xicanachronicles.com/platica_celeste_de_luna/. Accessed 15 Aug. 2016.

---. "Sleeping with the Enemy, Part I." *XicanaChronicles.com*, 5 June 2015, xicanachronicles.com/sleeping-with-the-enemy-part-i/. Accessed 4 Aug. 2016.

---. "Sleeping with the Enemy Part II." 5 Sept. 2015, xicanachronicles.com/sleeping-with-the-enemy-part-ii/. Accessed 5 Aug. 2016.

---. *South: Point of Entry*. 2012, acrylic on canvas, artist's private collection, La Ferria, Texas

---. *West: El Muro*. 2012, acrylic on canvas, artist's private collection, La Ferria, Texas.

Elizondo Griest, Stephanie. "Art Against the Wall." *Oxford American*, no. 88, Spring 2015, www.oxfordamerican.org/magazine/item/558-art-against-the-wall. Accessed 4 Aug. 2016.

---. *All the Agents and Saints: Dispatches from the U.S. Borderlands*. University of North Carolina, 2017.

Hopewell, Cameron. "CCA Reports First Quarter 2016 Financial Results." *GlobalNewsWire*.

*com*, 4 May 2016, www.globenewswire.com/news-release/2016/05/04/836807/0/en/CCA-Reports-First-Quarter-2016-Financial-Results.html. Accessed 29 Aug. 2016.

"Increase in Illegal Border Crossings Prompts Honduras To Open Consulate In South Texas." *Fox News*. 1 July 2013. Web. www.foxnews.com/politics/2013/07/01/increase-in-illegal-crossings-prompts-honduras-to-open-consulate-at-texas.html. Accessed 5 Aug. 2016.

"Nationally recognized Valley artist to exhibit, lecture during STC's Hispanic Heritage Month Celebration," *SouthTexasCollege.edu*. Last modified 14 Aug. 2013. http://news.southtexascollege.edu/?p=7090. Accessed 14 Aug. 2016.

Taylor, Steve. "Abbot makes border security a legislative priority." *Rio Grande Guardian*, 18 Feb. 2015, Web. riograndeguardian.com/abbott-makes-border-security-a-legislative-priority/. Accessed 14 Aug. 2016.

United States Customs and Immigration Department. Department of Homeland Security. *Vision and Strategy 2020, U.S. Customs and Border Protection Strategic Plan*. Mar. 2015. Web. Aug. 2016. www.cbp.gov/sites/default/files/documents/CBP-Vision-Strategy-2020.pdf

United States Department of Justice. *Highlights of the USA PATRIOT Act: The USA PATRIOT Act: Preserving Life and Liberty*. Web. Mar. 2015. www.justice.gov/archive/ll/what_is_the_patriot_act.pdf

"Witnessing surge of unaccompanied minors in McAllen, DHS chief declares emergency." *Monitor* [McAllen, TX]. Web. 17 May 2014, http://www.themonitor.com/news/local/witnessing-surge-of-unaccompanied-minors-in-mcallen-dhs-chief-declares/article_0f440394-de1f-11e3-ac37-0017a43b2370.html. Accessed 14 Aug. 2016.

# NEPANTLER@ TESTIMONIOS

## A DISCUSSION OF RISKING THE PERSONAL, TRAUMA, AND BORDER-CROSSING MOVEMENTS IN HIGHER EDUCATION

ITZEL CORONA AGUILAR, RICHARD GIDDENS, JR., SUSANA N. RAMÍREZ, MEGAN MICHELLE MORAN

Gloria E. Anzaldúa introduced the term "nepantleras" to describe cultural visionaries engaging in spiritual activism, "work[ing] from multiple locations," and "try[ing] to overturn the destructive perceptions of the world that we've been taught by our various cultures" ("Speaking" 293). The acts of moving between, within, and outside of multiple worlds shape the identities and experiences of nepantler@s.[1] Through this constant shifting, Anzaldúa's nepantler@s invite us to reimagine new spiritual and political subjectivities and epistemologies that "risk the personal," confront trauma, and heal generational wounds. By disclosing intimate details, beliefs, and emotions through our collective testimonios, we center the importance of what AnaLouise Keating calls "risking the personal" in Anzaldúa's nepantler@ work (Keating 2).

In the following four-part discussion, "Nepantler@ Testimonios" serve as deep inner work informing the outer political work of nepantler@s. Our collective testimonios are shaped by our previous scholarship on Anzaldúa, our experiences inside, between, and outside of academia, and healing from violence on our bodymindspirits. Throughout our multiple discussions, we realized that we were all reflecting on some form of spirituality and inner/outer work associated with the Four Directions—East, West, North, and South. We open with the direction of the East (new beginnings) with Itzel Corona Aguilar's testimonio as an undocumented graduate student. Aguilar presents a testimonio that demonstrates the reflexive and difficult process nepantler@ intellectuals often engage in to find profound healing from generational wounds. We turn to the direction of the West (endings) to release multiple interlocking traumas on the bodymindspirit through Richard Giddens, Jr.'s testimonio of surviving and thriving. Susana N. Ramírez directs us to the ancestral direction of the North, where she explores the lives of her parents shaping her nepantler@ identity between what often feel like contradictory worlds of indigenous curanderismo and academia. Last, we turn to the direction of the South with Megan Michelle Moran's testimonio. She draws on the unrelenting spirit of Huitzilopochtli as she finds solace in the words inscribed in books to grieve from her grandmother's recent passing. Together, we offer our testimonio ofrendas to the next seven generations of nepantler@ intellectuals.

## LA QUE EN EL CORRAL VIVE DE LA MIERDA SE ENAMORA

*Itzel Corona Aguilar*

### PREFACE

I write and I feel pain where my right kidney is. I have carried this pain for quite some time, but it was not until recently that I learned about the nation/state governance that my body had been subjected to as a young child. When I entered the US, I tested positive for tuberculosis (TB) because of a vaccine I received in México. In order to attend school, I needed to take TB medication for a year, which is known to be difficult on your kidneys—even for a grown adult. Yet there I was at 8 years old, cleansing myself y mi pobre riñón. I even remember the pulsating headaches. After many years passed, I learned that those were some of the symptoms of the medication. Mi madre, sin hablar inglés, asks herself: how could she have known how to navigate that system? Mi cuerpecito, apenas empezando a crecer and already being subjected to anti-immigrant invasive cleanses. What if my body was expected to become a vessel of governance that needed nationhood to thrive? Mi cuerpo, igual como el de mi madre, would always be subjected to political control outside of my own. The biometrics of my life would forever remain a capsule of me. Who I am is easily accessible to el hielo. My poor kidney carries all this pain; it is the organ of my memories.

### *YO SOY LA MAGNA LUZ ELECTRÓNICA QUE ENTRA Y FLUYE POR CADA CELULA DE MI CUERPO*

The day of and after my wedding, my kidney pulsated. Me dolía un chingo. At moments, I thought it would burst. Each pulsation of pain was a reminder of a memory I had forgotten. Each memory pierces the area in my brain that reads and reacts to pain. I feel this pain when I write, and, although I have lived with this pain for many years, it was not until I started applying to graduate school and situating myself in the academic world that my kidney began to revolt. My kidney vocalized her disapproval much louder than I ever expected, but I strategically ignored her gritos. My right kidney carries trauma—a trauma situated in the space of rejection that constantly attempts to dim the luz of my being. My relationship to academia, like many of my relationships with loved ones, has always been poisonous. I grew up seeing pain. The luchadoras in my life have been deeply wounded by ex-partners, and their stories, along with mine, only become harder to bear as I get older. I do not know what a healthy life looks like. My relationship with academia is nourished through unhealthy acts of masochism and a constant concern with not being enough and being too much at the same time. How can my relationship with academia thrive when I have never known how healthy love looks and feels?

When I was hospitalized after trying to take my life, my kidney started screaming. It was 12:00 AM when I woke up feeling the menacing pain in my side, except, this time, the pain started from my lower back all the way around to my belly button. I asked to see the doctor on call, and he checked me out. He said there was nothing wrong with me, and asked, "Why are you lying?" I held my side, wishing I could disappear into and within the pain—a profound pain that pierced my kidney through every breath of desperation I took. My fever started to rise, and I was rushed to a different hospital. Ella me estaba tratando de ayudar. Sus gritos se convirtieron en memorias del pasado, past traumas, and memories of times when I had been hurt. These memories were sharp as a blade. Sus gritos me dijeron que necesitaba salir de ahí. I needed to get out of the hospital. I needed to come home to San Anto, Tejas. It was time to start listening.

The entire time I was in the hospital, I convinced myself that I was not supposed to be there—this allowed me to survive. I quickly trained my body to ignore the pain of my pobre riñón, but I also trained my ears to ignore the gritos from the other patients. The cries for help. Los llantos de dolor. Cries of help that screeched through the silence. Llantos that we could feel internally through an interconnected level that was incredibly frightening. I tried to push out the noises in my own head by convincing myself that it was all a mistake, but the reality of my current situation was far more complex than I was willing to recognize. I lied to myself, pero mi riñón me recordaba que no iba ser tan fácil escapar el pasado. I spent six days at the hospital. Seis largos días—los más largos de mi vida.

I would sleep and whimper out of pain but never shed a tear. I couldn't. I had already cried too much before I arrived at the hospital. I had spent days crying all day thinking of how to leave my life, a life that I stopped treasuring because the spaces I was in made me feel insignificant. I have spent years struggling with depression, and it is within the ivory walls of the academic tower that those feelings resurfaced y La Coatlicue finalmente ganó. I was in pain, not just because of past trauma pero también porque mi voz no era suficiente. My depression is built on violence.

> *Voy cagándome de miedo, buscando lugares acuevados.* I don't want to know. I don't want to be seen. My resistance, my refusal to know some truth about myself brings on that paralysis, depression—brings on the *Coatlicue* state. At first I feel exposed and opened to the depth of my dissatisfaction. Then I feel myself closing, hiding, holding myself together rather than allowing myself to fall apart. (Anzaldúa, *Borderlands* 70)

When I would enter the classroom, I would freeze. El hielo corría por cada celula de mi cuerpo. I could not speak. I would spend the entire class time, all three hours, thinking about how to speak. I had to re-learn how to use my tongue because, in these spaces, los movimientos de mi lengua paraban de funcionar. My tongue could not function because, symbolically, it had been cut out. My tongue was a sacrificial offering to the gods when I was accepted into this graduate program. Now, I need to grow it back—but this time with espinas de nopal, thick and sharp, so I can navigate these toxic systems that dim la luz de mi ser.

> *Soy nopal de castilla* like the spineless and therefore defenseless cactus that Mamagrande Ramona grew in back of her shed. I have no protection. So I cultivate needles, nettles, razor-sharp spikes to protect myself from others (67).

I left the hospital with an awareness of how I had perceived love. It was a deeply political and perverse love that manifested itself through acts of masochism upon my being. When I write, I torture myself. When I was in the hospital, I wrote. I wrote because, in my eyes, I was already dead. I had nothing else to lose. This torture always leads to healing—it is a path I have come to love. What if the energy behind my masochist tendencies can be transformed into a loving capability that leads to healing? What if I can put this poison to use? What if I can convert it to ink para escribir mixed with sangre de mi corazón con razón? When I was in the hospital I had to re-learn how to write. I wrote with my heart.

These relationships have been founded on love. A love for pain. My relationship with academia is complex due to its constant rejection and stimulation of me. I am constantly seeking a space where my voice is not only heard but also supported and entertained. I desire for my voice to be heard without the immediate assumption that I am speaking from a place of hostility. I wanted academia to care about me, and I sought acceptance the way you seek love from an unhealthy partner who constantly rejects and insults you. These are the types of relationships I have always known. Mi madre me dice la que en el corral vive de la mierda se enamora. And through her being I begin to understand. I begin to understand that I am that gallina living in the corral, falling in love with shit. I am constantly committing to partners that enact violence upon my being. Although this violence is always emotional, it is no stranger to the pressure and pain of a gaping wound. I have felt that violence, and I have also become that violent.

My first year of grad school was similar to loving an abusive partner. I was in an abusive relationship with academia, and, regardless of all of my efforts, I was not enough. I am still not enough, and, in the moments when I do expose myself, I am always too much. Throughout my first year, I experienced a violence that converted mi lengua into an insignificant organ with no purpose—an organ that is unable to function to its full radical potential. I am that gallina running around como loca sin lengua para gritar.

## NEPANTLER@ RESEARCHER (RE)VIEWING & (RE)MEMBERING SELF: QUEER TEJAN@ TESTIMONIO AS METHOD AND SELF-CARE

*Richard Giddens, Jr.*

I burn copal and call upon the ancestral spirits of the West to guide the endings of life's traumas that allow growth of mindbodyspirit and, specifically, the ancestral spirit of mi abuela, Oralia Flores Hernández, who continues to walk by my side.

My experiences living as a light-skinned, queer Tejan@ (I use the @ to denote a queer ethnic identity) /Xican@ in San Antonio, Texas, have been, and continue to be, fraught. When I entered the Texas public school system through Southwest Elementary in the fall of 1986, I immediately understood I had to keep my queer identity a secret, while living in constant fear that my performed façade of hetero-masculinity would crack, allowing my sissy demeanor to shine. I grew up in an annexed township incorporated into San Antonio and Bexar County called Von Ormy, or "V.O." as the local kids of my generation refer to it, named after the Counts Von Ormay of Hungary, Texas, and Brazil. Interstate Highway 35-South is still my family's view from the front yard. Some of my uncles were truck drivers, so whenever we saw one drive by, we would wave as though it were one of them. With train tracks, a Texaco truck stop in walking distance, and the Medina River less than a five-minute walk past, I explored and became an expert in the geography and bucolic yet urbanized spaces of my hometown. To say I was bullied because I was an effeminate boy would be accurate.

Growing up queer, I knew I didn't fit in, and I was queer at multiple intersections. I wasn't brown enough, or Mexican enough, nor taught to speak Spanish by my parents and grandparents, who were all fluent. My generation of the Hernández/Flores clan was raised as Texan (white) as the two-story-high pecan tree my grandfather planted in the back yard when my mother was born. My grandma would tell us stories of how, when she was a little girl, she and her siblings would be corporally punished if they were caught speaking Spanish in school. Assimilation was a survival strategy that, combined with the Irish-immigrant last name of my great-grandfather on my dad's side, allowed the bullies to erase any sense of my Tejanidad (Tejano or Mexican Texan identity) by policing my racial identity away from the brown and into the white. The white bullies were no better. To them, I wasn't man enough. I was a sissy, a faggot, a gay-lord, and whatever else they heard their bigoted parents yell at the television the night before. I remember places, school, family gatherings, events at Sacred Heart of Jesus Catholic Church where the kids routinely passed the time beating each other. This was one of the main reasons that I avoided boys, and had only made friends with girls. Another reason was that I was always dealt the task of getting beat. This game was called "smear the queer." Whoever was holding the ball, or whomever the other kids wanted/needed a reason to pick on, was chased, tackled and humiliated with taunts of being the queer who got smeared. Looking back on my childhood, it's clear: the politicized, queer, Tejan@/Xican@, scholar-activist I became was inadvertently constructed by institutionalized homophobia and heteropatriarchy, while my gender performance remained policed by a never-ending parade of hyper-masculinized, gay-bashing boys of every color.

At the beginning of my thirty-fifth year, in March 2016, I was preparing to begin my first research project. I also began to experience what seemed like a post-adolescent mental, somatic, and spiritual mindbodyspirit growth spurt. Along with this new sensitivity came bodily stresses in the form of unexplained fevers, sweats, enigmatic dreams of my deceased abuela, and sleep paralysis nightmares. The fevers were curious, only occurring during sleep. Within an hour or two of waking, they would break. Intuition told me this was a spiritual pathology. Because of this newly heightened susceptibility to corporeal ailment, for the first time in my life I met with a practicing curandera for a ritual limpia/spiritual cleansing. Relying on my Xican@ academic connections, I was led to the care of Erika Casasola, a local San Antonio practicing curandera. At our meeting, I first informed Erika (my healer/teacher) that I sought her out because my personal efforts at spiritual cleansings, which had always proven efficient in the past, were no longer working. She asked me where I learned to use the medicine, the practice of curanderismo. I didn't have a definitive answer to this query; the intuition had always been there. Next I explained a perplexing dream I had about mi abuela.

Grandma Ora (Oralia), who passed away in the winter of late 2014, was sitting in a bed. The room was brightly lit in a cosmic white light, and the only color was my grandmother's. She called me to her, but the only words I understood were "Mijo, come here." She took my two hands into hers, and held them very tightly. Entonces, like a whirlwind, she began to speak in a rapid yet fastidious manner, entirely en español. I pleaded with her to slow down, because my Tex-Mex/Spanglish language abilities couldn't keep up with what she was saying. She was well aware that my generation of the family wasn't raised fluently bilingual. As quickly as it began, the dream was over, and I awoke in a pool of my own sweat with a fever of 102 degrees.

After sharing this dream and a plática lasting half an hour, my healer/teacher informed me that a limpia was not what I needed. What I was suffering from was a supersaturating of negative energies and I needed assistance filtering and grounding these malignancies. What I heard next validated something I felt I'd always known, though it still shocked me. "You're a healer," she said. I thought I was sick because of some outside force imposing sickness upon me, but in fact, I was ill because I'd absorbed an abundance of negative energy from people, places, and objects my entire life. I was entirely unaware of bioenergetics and the fact that I was particularly susceptible. The (re)viewing and (re)membering of my sexual assault trauma as part of my research was also a factor. My prescription combined the acknowledgment of this ancestral gift with the embracing of the medicine, followed by a blessing of strength to boost my spiritual immune system. During my strength blessing, Erika noticed there was a staunch blockage within my solar plexus. In my mind, it appeared like a jet-black hockey puck lodged within my core. After a while of concentrated energy manipulation, the hockey puck broke open, and my stiff body fell limp to the floor. On the way down, mi abuela came to me, and, as though she were back at her position in the Von Ormy Post Office, she delivered a memory parcel to my consciousness. I remembered that as a baby, my grandmother practiced curanderismo whenever I had a fever, the hiccups, or a stomach ache. Grandma Ora is my connection to the medicine, and in the dream she was trying to tell me this. She was trying to tell me that my gifts are in my hands.

There was a particular event, un arrebato, as Chicana feminist theorist Gloria Anzaldúa termed it: a violent susto that "turns your world upside down and cracks the walls of your reality, resulting in a great sense of loss, grief, and emptiness, leaving behind dreams, hopes, and goals. You are no longer who you used to be" (*Light* 125). Mi arrebato occured the night I was sexually assaulted by two men after they force-fed me a bottle of wine laced with their date-rape drug of choice.

It was the shock from this arrebato that led to my current path in academia and the social sciences. When I transferred to the University of Texas at San Antonio in 2013 to complete my undergraduate studies, I was doing so as a method to heal from emotional and psychological injuries and trauma from el arrebato. What I learned as a student in the Women's Studies Program at UTSA transformed my understanding and critique of my life growing up queer, light-skinned, and from an Americanized Tejano family in San Antonio, Tejas. This new insight into the world systems of institutionalized cis-heteropatriarchy, racism, and capitalism now fueled my research as a scholar-activist. It was the writings of US Third World feminist theorists like Anzaldúa, Audre Lorde, and Cherríe Moraga, among others, who teach us to write our bodies and lived experiences existing in our uniquely marginalized spaces, those in-between spaces Anzaldúa terms "nepantla." My work reflects my existence as a nepantler@, an inhabitant of that in-between space, and centers around healing through the power of testimonio, performance, and the production of what Chicana literary and cultural critics Moraga and Anzaldúa have termed "theory in the flesh" (*This Bridge* 19).

While at UTSA, my understanding of why I set out on this mission was disclosed. First, I needed to be here to heal myself. Second, I yearned to serve as a conduit of healing for others who cross my path in life, the academy, and activism. I plan on continuing these pursuits in my graduate studies at the

University of Cambridge, England, with particular emphasis on the praxis of Queer Chicana feminist thought to galvanize social equity, and add queer temporal representation to the current heteronormative literary canon.

My research combines decolonial qualitative methods, ethnography, and queer theory, and is titled "(Re)viewing & (Re)membering Violence: Testimonios of Queer & Trans Tejan@x Sexual Assault Experiences." I critique the current state of sexual assault resources available in San Antonio and the lack of these healing spaces exclusively marketed to Queer and/or Trans Tejan@x people. The experience I've gained by taking on this groundbreaking project of social justice importance has been traumatic in itself. In (re)viewing & (re)membering mi arrebato, I was reminded that "you gotta do the work" to "let us be the healing of the wound." I have learned that there's always room for improvement when approaching research from a new perspective or non-normative paradigm, such as indigenous/decolonial thought and testimonio as method. I have also learned that you cannot get discouraged when plans fail, or when they transform into new knowledge that was never intended. After all, that's research.

In closing, I give thanks to my Grandma Ora(lia) for walking this path of healing with me, always watching over me from the other side, to Gloria Evangelina Anzaldúa for teaching me that healing is possible even within the confinements of white cishetero academia, and to the ancestors for the blood and energy that fuel mi corazón y los corazónes de mi jotería hermosa.

## NEPANTLERA INTELLECTUAL: BRIDGING INDIGENOUS CURANDERISMO AND ACADEMIC SPLITS

*Susana N. Ramírez*

I call upon the ancestral spirits of the North with photographs of my mother, Maria Guadalupe Ramírez, ironically resisting a hug from my grandmother at the Basilica of La Virgen de Guadalupe in México City, and my father Jose

**Figure 1. Photograph with my grandma & mom**

**Figure 2. Photograph of my dad**

Ramírez Velasco, whose connection to his mother lives on through spirit form. Here, in the ivory walls of academia, their brown faces declare: "we are still here." Despite every colonial effort of erasure, we are still here. Because I am still here.

## NEPANTLERA INTELLECTUAL FORMATIONS

I am a capirotada (sweet bread) product of those before me who gave life to the nepantlera intellectual: Dr. Susana N. Ramírez. From my father, I carry the indigenous medicine of my grandmother, Matiana Velasco, otherwise known as "la bruja" in the family who possessed the gift of premonition and a deep connection with Mother Earth. I learned to listen to Madre Tierra, too, and her profound teachings: to look to the trees shedding their leaves in the autumn to rebirth them again in the spring; to return to water to feel profound wholeness; to lose the fear of the fire of my center; and to listen to the messages of the winds evoking new changes. Through my father's oral stories, I woke up from a long self-destructive sleep. From my mother, I learned my passion for education and the transformative potential of the classroom environment. She is the same mother who dropped out of elementary school to care for her nine siblings, but who also inspired in me the ganas to reach the finish line: PhD. A feat reserved for only 0.2% of those who look like me. More importantly, she taught me the magic of words on a page serving as healing "hierbitas or curing stones" transforming the ailments of the soul like the writings of literary curandera Gloria E. Anzaldúa ("Metaphors" 122).

I would become my parents' bridge between the two worlds: indigenous curanderismo and academia. More importantly, I would offer nepantlera intellectual tactics of transformation that point to this illusive division. Nepantlera intellectuals draw those interconnections: burning sage to cleanse our work offices, publishing research *con corazón* asserting the significance of indigenous healing arts and health care systems, and offering healing círculos to university students who have survived sexual assault and trauma. But nothing would foment this bridging like those last few months of finishing my dissertation.

> *I am FUCKING D-O-N-E! I never want to go through that again! Today I heard myself telling myself that my dissertation was a failure and my advisor would not approve it. I contemplated suicide if she did not.*
>
> –Journal entry, December 18, 2016

How did I get to this point? When did my dissertation become more important than my own life? These are questions that led me to a weeklong apprenticeship with curandera elder Rita Navarette Pérez in México City in February 2016. I arrived to Temazcal Tonatiuh, her healing center, feeling so small, broken, and fragmented. Through a dramatic shift in my diet, two intense temazcales (sweat lodges), and two sobadas (profound energetic massages), I learned more about my ancestral wounds. We returned to my childhood and confronted trauma of domestic violence in my family. This unlatched an unrelenting rage I held onto for several years towards my mother. My child self could not understand how someone who had shared a heartbeat with me left me so alone to confront my father's alcoholism. Later, my adult self would understand that my mother also split from herself in those moments of trauma to survive and give us the best life she could give us. As part of my healing, though, I released the toxic anger from my bodymindspirit in its full fury to then pick myself up physically, spiritually, and emotionally from the ground. I stopped waiting to be saved. I saved myself and became my own curandera with the guidance of abuela Rita.

While in México, I also realized that much of my experiences with depression and mental illness in academia reflected accumulated pain stored over the years inside my chest area without a place to go. In academia, you are encouraged to be hyperproductive, machine-like while undergoing daily insults to the bodymindspirit, also known as microaggressions. Luckily, abuela Rita helped me release that pain through an intense sobada that left me screaming and crying in the moment. While releasing was painful, more dreadful was the thought of storing this pain in my bodymindspirit that could manifest later in chronic congestion, depression, and/or at worst, cancer. I chose to let go of the rage as a gift to myself. I had convinced myself that depression was a "normal" part of everyday life. No. Who robbed us of our powerful ancestral medicine and rituals? I chose to leave my pain and chose to relate to my mother and myself differently.

When the rage began to dissolve, I realized that my training in academia gave me the language to talk about my experiences with my mother beyond a "malinche" individual who made poor decisions. I looked to Chicana feminist theorist Eden E. Torres whose discussions of PTSD reminded me that these wounds go way back. This allowed me to be compassionate towards my mother. We carry these wounds in on our bodymindspirits through each generation, hoping nobody will uncover them. And yet, here I was poking and prodding because I desperately needed to heal for the next seven generations and for myself. My life depended on it. Furthermore, my academic Chicana feminist training gave me the words to understand my mother's decision working against multiple interlocking systemic oppressions: an undocumented brown working-class woman who only spoke Spanish. She needed to cut off the experience of her child getting physically abused to provide what she perceived as a better life. What other options did she have? Does it make sense? No. But these are the realities of many undocumented people living in the shadows.

It is all connected. That is the work of the nepantlera intellectuals—to help us see those connections. We remind folks that these splits and walls are illusionary and that, in fact, they were never split. I am still learning how to balance what feels like opposite, contradictory worlds at times, but I insist and dream of that cosmic possibility. And yet, I know that I am neither the first nor the only one bridging these worlds together. Thank you to the nepantlera intellectuals before me, with me, and those who will come after me. I see you, I love you. Thank you, especially to my parents, my first teachers of ancestral resilience and bridgework.

## "MIJA, YOUR EDUCATION IS SO IMPORTANT": DECOLONIZING THE EDUCATION SYSTEM

*Megan Michelle Moran*

When I am beyond consolable and seeking light in my life, I go to my bookcase and pull *Making Face, Making Soul/Haciendo Caras* from the shelf. I'll embrace the book for a few seconds, and then, open to the poem "Poem For The Young White Man Who Asked Me How I, An Intelligent, Well-Read Person, Could Believe In The War Between Races," by Lorna Dee Cervantes. The poem is not soothing by any means, but instead, creates a sense of urgency begging the reader to act now and act quickly. The feeling of urgency is why I read this poem time and time again—it reminds me who I am, where I came from, and causes me to channel any negative energy into productivity. Cervantes's poem begs me to think of those who have influenced my life, and my grandmother always comes to mind as a woman of strength and perseverance.

My grandmother, Rebecca Hernandez Moran, took her last breath on this Earth recently. She died traumatically after the nursing staff at her nursing home dropped her and broke both of her legs. Our family opted to do surgery even though it was not likely she would make it through due to her age and fragile state. She survived. Not long after, she was put into hospice care, and we watched her slowly wither away as she had not eaten since the night she broke her legs. Our family surrounded her each day, pushing through with her, and comforting her in any way we could. Like the true survivor she is, she pushed until the very last second. She told us to take care of each other, and love one another. The last true conversation we had was when she was in the hospital just before her surgery, "Mija, take care of yourself and be a good little girl." She blessed me and we hugged as my heart broke. She and I both knew deep down this was the last time we would speak. The morning she died, I curled up in bed and cried while holding my book knowing it was the only thing that could comfort me.

When I think of the stories she would tell me, I would imagine her life played out in black and white. My grandma was a true Rosie the Riveter and worked at Kelly Airfield during WWII. She raised six children, five boys and one girl, the oldest being my father, Virgilio, who was named after his father. She was a strict woman, but loving and kind. She taught me how to braid my hair as we watched her novelas in the living room on her couch with a plastic covering, so it would never get dirty. She loved sewing and made clothing for all of my dolls out of recycled scrap material, and, each night, when it was time for bed, we would lie side by side and pray the Rosary in Spanish.

Something my grandmother always instilled in me and her other sixteen grandchildren was to receive an education: "Mija, your education is so important, something nobody can take away from you." Throughout my years in school, I carried those words with me, and, when I thought I would fail (and sometimes when I did), I would hear her speaking to me and would persevere. In times of loneliness, panic, or sadness, I would start to pray the Rosary just as she taught me. I sometimes prayed in the middle of class, drowning out the words of professors. Something nobody ever tells you about being a Mexican-American woman who receives a college education is that so often the people who are rooting for you the most will never benefit from your education. We see this issue often in the women's studies community—how will you help your community if your community does not have basic access to education? We are trying so hard to reach our people, but how do we accomplish this enormous task when the education system was not built for people of color?

We must decolonize the education system. Right now, our education system is oppressing people of color. We are not in textbooks; the enforcers of ideologies are people in power—the white man. The white man must suppress others in order to remain in power. Oppression is a tactic used by oppressors to keep marginalized people down in order to keep power in favor of the oppressor. The oppressor tells us to change ourselves. They say we are too brown, do not speak "proper" English, call us dirty, and spit in our faces. To decolonize we must unlearn everything we have learned, and this is no small feat.

About three years ago I was doing local research at the Institute of Texan Cultures, digging up information regarding alternate histories on the San Antonio Missions. The archives are only so helpful; I sifted through several boxes only to find a limited number of documents to assist in my research. The majority of what has been written is based on whitewashed histories, histories written only by those in power. I think about the time I discovered an article on the first textbook in Texas. The textbook was written by a man who was in charge of indigenous people at one of the San Antonio Missions. In the article the author describes how to "control" and "civilize" Native Americans. As I sat in the archive reading this document, my immediate response was anger, and, quickly following, disbelief. I had always known the education system was corrupt—my other grandmother would spend hours talking to my cousin and me about disparities among people of color. These narratives often related to spaces of oppression like the Missions. After all, these spaces are in the I-grew-up-in-San-Antonio rites-of-passage field trips to sites of genocide. Holding the document in my hands—reading the same words used tactically to oppress—made everything very concrete. It is clear from the start: our education system reinforces colonial history.

For Chicanas, it is especially difficult to unlearn what colonialism has taught us, because we are oppressed not only culturally, but also as mujeres. We live between two universes, wanting to be in solidarity with Chicanos, but we are not male, no matter if we face the same struggles culturally within white politics. While Chicanos can help uplift us, they can just as quickly suppress us as women. This is a direct result of colonialism, reinforcing the notion that men are superior to women. It has been ingrained in us to hate our culture and ourselves. As Chican@s, colonizers have conditioned us to do to ourselves what the oppressor does to us—this is neocolonization. We internalize the oppressions on ourselves and react toward others facing similar oppressions. This is the objective of the colonizer: for us to internalize our own self-hatred. We are in constant rivalry with our counterparts who are oppressed. We learn not to trust our own raza because of our differences.

Marginalized people are pitted against each other because of our differences. Internalized colonization is a newer form of colonialism where we self-police each other, doing what the oppressor has done to us (Adams 55). We look down on those who choose to step outside the boundaries that were assigned to us by colonizers. This gap is used as a strategic method: it causes people of color to focus on our differences instead of working together. This is where the education gap comes into play and the question arises, how do we help our communities if we are being pitted against each other? It is difficult to express the extent to which we are being pitted against one another because the ways are endless and overwhelming. The primary step to begin decolonizing education is to first acknowledge my privilege as an educated Chicana and then to focus all work on the community. This will hopefully begin to make the gap between academia and community smaller.

For Chican@s, the questioning of the education system is important to our existence because, when we question systems, we are also questioning the patriarchal values that stemmed from history. We can question the colonialism, the neocolonialism (which we impose onto ourselves and others), and the internalized racism and sexism. Decolonizing ourselves is a difficult process and is not something that can occur overnight. It will likely take years, possibly centuries to disentangle. It will take unlearning tactics imposed on us by colonizers, but eventually enforced through neocolonization.

This brings me back to my grandmother, because it is from her resilience and strength that I was able to make it through the education system. In many ways, we carry our family with us through college. We make caldo to cure colds, we light prayer candles before our exams, we soothe our souls with elote. Now I only pray to give back to the community who raised me because my grandmother did not make all of her sacrifices for nothing. I will continue to question the system, the dominant culture, and the white man. Undoing colonialism will be the greatest struggle, yet we cannot give up our fight or give in to patriarchy.

## CONCLUSION

We give thanks to the four directions for holding space for us to use the power of word to heal. As nepantler@ intellectuals, we are committed to the project of love that is required to decolonize the space of academia. We navigate the ivory tower through a US Third World politics that builds on a toolkit of resistance with a commitment to build and nurture spaces we have long been pushed out of. We call on the forces of our ancestors and those that walk with us even if we are not aware of their presence. We call on the love of our mothers and abuelitas who, for centuries, sacrificed their lives to ensure that we could live our own. We also challenge the histories we carry within our veins as we recreate history through the testimonios we narrate.

## NOTES

1. While Anzaldúa uses the term "nepantlera," we use "nepantler@" to include people from multiple genders. We find relevant Sandra K. Soto's description of the @ suffix symbol. See Soto 2–3.

## WORKS CITED

Adams, Howard. *Tortured People: The Politics of Colonization.* Theytus Books Ltd., 1999.

Anzaldúa, Gloria. *Borderlands/La Frontera: The New Mestiza.* 1987. Aunt Lute. 4th edition, 2012.

---. *Light in the Dark/Luz en lo Oscuro: Rewriting Identity, Spirituality, Reality*, edited by AnaLouise Keating, Duke UP, 2015.

---. "Metaphors in the Tradition of the Shaman." *The Gloria Anzaldúa Reader*, edited by AnaLouise Keating, Duke UP, 2009, pp. 121–23.

---. "Speaking across the Divide." *The Gloria Anzaldúa Reader*, edited by AnaLouise Keating, Duke UP, 2009, pp. 282–94.

Keating, AnaLouise. "Risking the Personal: An Introduction." *Interviews/Entrevistas*, edited by AnaLouise Keating, Routledge, 2000, pp. 1–15.

Moraga, Cherríe, and Gloria E. Anzaldúa, eds. *This Bridge Called My Back: Writings by Radical Women of Color*. 4th ed. State U of New York P, 2015.

Soto, Sandra K. *Reading Chican@ Like A Queer: The De-Mastery of Desire.* U of Texas P, 2010.

# CONTRIBUTOR BIOGRAPHIES

**Norma Alarcón**, cultural philosopher, literary critic, editor, translator, writer. Best known for being a central referent in Chicana feminism. Professor emerita from the Ethnic Studies Department at the University of California, Berkeley. She was the founder of Third Woman Press. Some of her publications include *The Poetics of Difference in the Work of Rosario Castellanos* (published also in a self-translation in Spanish), "Chicana Feminism: In the tracks of 'the' Native Woman," "The Theoretical Subject(s) of *This Bridge Called My Back*," and other well-known works.

**Marisa Belausteguigoitia**, Full Professor at the School of Humanities at the UNAM/México D.F. She analyzes the relation of critical pedagogies, art, and justice from a gender perspective in women's prisons. Author of numerous books. Her work has been recognized with awards, such as the 2015 Best Film and Best Director at the FICFUSA festival in Colombia for the documentary *Nos pintamos solas*. Her last co-edited book, *Critical Terms in Caribbean and Latin American Thought*, was dedicated to her friend and advisor Norma Alarcón.

**Itzel Corona Aguilar** is a doctoral student at Rutgers University and alumna of the University of Texas at San Antonio. Born in Mexico City, Corona Aguilar came to the US with her family when she was seven years old. She says that being an undocumented immigrant is a large part of her identity.

Named "Best of San Antonio Local Author," **Anel I. Flores** has been awarded the Chingona in Literature Award, Ancinas at Squaw Valley Award, National Association of Latino Arts and Cultures (NALAC) Fund for the Arts Award, Acción Women Inspiring Women Award, Yellow Rose of Texas Educator Award, and the Mentorship Leadership award from the National Performance Network. She is co-editor of the *Jota Anthology* and author of Lambda Literary Award–nominated *Empanada*. Flores holds an MFA in creative writing, and is a member of Macondo Writer's Workshop, the Society for the Study of Gloria Anzaldúa, and NALAC.

**Richard Giddens, Jr.** is a Queer Tejan@ Nepantler@ academic from Von Ormy, Texas, a graduate of the Women's Studies Institute at the University of Texas at San Antonio, and is pursuing his MPhil and future PhD in multidisciplinary gender studies at Peterhouse, University of Cambridge, England. He plans on following in the footsteps of his Xican@ feminist academic mentors in the fight to decolonize academia.

**Yndalecio Isaac Hinojosa** is an assistant professor of English at Texas A&M University–Corpus Christi and co-editor of *Open Words: Access and English Studies*. His work focuses on intersections between Chicana third space feminist theory and writing studies under the lenses of border theory, gender, sexuality, nationality, and race.

**Jennifer Lozano**, like Gloria Anzaldúa, was raised in the Rio Grande Valley and is influenced by its rich and complex mestizo culture. After obtaining a BA in English from Texas A&M University, she went on to complete a MA from Kansas State University and a PhD from the University of Illinois, Urbana-Champaign. Her primary research focuses on spirituality, neoliberalism, and transnational Latino/a identity and experience in contemporary Latina/o literature and culture. She is also interested in women of color feminism, women and gender studies, digital media studies, "global" literature, and 20th- and 21st-century American literature and culture, especially literature of the Southwest. The work and life of Anzaldúa continues to be a source of intellectual and political growth for her and her work. Jennifer is currently an assistant professor of Latina/o literature and culture at the University of North Carolina, Wilmington.

**Larissa M. Mercado-López** received her PhD in English literature at the University of Texas at San Antonio. She is currently an associate professor of women's studies at California State University, Fresno, where she teaches courses on women of color feminisms and Latina health. She is the co-editor of several works, including three volumes of *El Mundo Zurdo*, and collections of critical essays on Latinx and Chicanx children's literature. Mercado-López is also a children's book author.

**Isabel Millán** is an assistant professor in the Department of American Ethnic Studies at Kansas State University with a PhD in American culture from the University of Michigan. She specializes in Chicana/o studies, critical ethnic studies, transnational feminist and queer theories, bilingual children's cultural productions, comics, and science fiction. Her recent publications include chapters in *Graphic Borders: Latino Comics Past, Present, and Future* and *The Routledge Companion to Latina/o Popular Culture*, as well as articles in *Signs: Journal of Women in Culture and Society* and *Aztlán: A Journal of Chicano Studies.*

**Megan Michelle Moran** studied at the University of Texas at San Antonio in the Women's Studies program and developed a deep passion for Chicana feminism, decolonial thought, and immigrant issues. She has a calling for community organizing. She has worked with End Family Detention to pass a resolution that would end detention for women and children. In Spring 2015, the UTSA organization she was a founding member of, Feminist@s Unite, won the UTSA President's Distinguished Diversity Award.

**Romana Radlwimmer** is an academic instructor and investigator at the Universities of Salamanca, Lisbon, and Missouri/Kansas City since 2009, focusing on Spanish/Latin American/Lusophone literatures/cultural studies. PhD in Latin American literature (University of Vienna) in 2012. Her monograph *Shifting Knowledges* was published in 2015 by the German editorial Königshausen & Neumann. Currently Assistant Professor at the Chair for Spanish Literatures at the University of Augsburg/Germany.

**Alejandra I. Ramírez** is currently a doctoral student at the University of Arizona, Tucson. She is a single parent to two young children. She spends most of her time thinking and writing, photographing the world around her, and painting abstract images of her dreamscapes. You can find her singing rancheras at a local restaurant; jumping into rivers, lakes, and oceans; or staring intently into the cosmos.

**Susana N. Ramírez**, PhD, is a queer nepantlera visionary, scholar, educator, and community sanadora living in San Antonio, Texas. She is a first-generation college student who recently earned her PhD in English (2016) while teaching women's studies and English courses at the University of Texas at San Antonio. As her life calling, she is a practitioner of Mexican traditional medicine (MTM) and indigenous ceremony.

**Sara A. Ramírez**, Post-Doctoral Associate in Chicano and Latino studies at the University of Minnesota, earned her PhD from the University of California, Berkeley. Her interdisciplinary research focuses on representations of historical and intergenerational trauma in Chicanx cultural productions. She has taught women's studies courses at the University of Texas at San Antonio. She is also the first member of a national collective working to revitalize the historic Third Woman Press.

**Fabiane Ramos** is a Brazilian-Australian adult educator with experience teaching languages and learning skills in Australia and South America. She has recently submitted her PhD thesis, a project about the migration and educational experiences of refugee-background youth in Australia, at the University of Queensland. In this work, she engages with Anzaldúa's writings/theories as the guiding soul informing her methodology and writing practices.

**Sonia Saldívar-Hull** is a professor of English and the founding director of the Women's Studies Institute and the Women's Studies Program at the University of Texas, San Antonio. Her publications include *Feminism on the Border: Chicana Feminist Politics and Literature*, and multiple book chapters and articles on Gloria Anzaldúa, Sandra Cisneros, and Helena María Viramontes, among others. Since 1997, she has been the co-editor of the book series *Latin America Otherwise*, published by Duke University Press.

**Veronica Sandoval** is Lady Mariposa, a graduate student at Washington State University working on her PhD in American studies. Her research interest includes Chola Praxis, Chicana feminism, global feminism, queer studies, the prison–industrial complex, immigration policies, and affect theory. She is a spoken-word artist who has been writing and performing poetry for over seventeen years. Her work has been published by Aunt Lute Books, the University of Delaware, Lamar University Press, Texas A&M University Press, and VAO Publishing.

**Candace Zepeda** is an assistant professor of English and the Director of QUEST First-Year Programs at Our Lady of the Lake University in San Antonio, Texas. She earned her PhD from the University of Texas at San Antonio in English, concentrating in rhetorical theory and Latin@ literary and cultural studies. Her current research interest focuses on how Hispanic-Serving Institutions are "serving" their population of students with the implementation of intentional programs, curriculum, and pedagogies.

**Aunt Lute Books** is a multicultural women's press that has been committed to publishing high-quality, culturally diverse literature since 1982. In 1990, the Aunt Lute Foundation was formed as a non-profit corporation to publish and distribute books that reflect the complex truths of women's lives and to present voices that are underrepresented in mainstream publishing. We seek work that explores the specificities of the very different histories from which we come, and the possibilities for personal and social change.

You may buy books from our website or by phoning in a credit card order.

www.auntlute.com

Aunt Lute Books
P.O. Box 410687
San Francisco, CA 94141
415.826.1300
books@auntlute.com

This book would not have been possible without the kind contributions of the Aunt Lute Founding Friends:

Anonymous Donor
Anonymous Donor
Rusty Barcelo
Marian Bremer
Marta Drury
Diane Goldstein
Diana Harris
Phoebe Robins Hunter
Diane Mosbacher, M.D., Ph.D.
Sara Paretsky
William Preston, Jr.
Elise Rymer Turner